The Ultimate Keto Bible with Pictures [4 Books in 1]

Cook and Taste Thousands of Low-Carb Dishes, Meal Preps, Snacks, Desserts… Follow the Smart Meal Plan Designed to Inspire Health, Shed Weight and Maintain It

By
Jamie Carter

Author : Jamie Carter

Jamie Carter is a nutritionist who specializes in the ketogenic diet and exercise physiology in 2015. He struggled with his health and her weight in childhood which led to her becoming such a passionate nutrition expert. "My goal is to help transform people lives and start living again!" Jamie spends most of his time with clients around the world via online coaching with amazing and measurable results. She specializes in helping autoimmune diseases, diabetes (type 1 and type 2), heart disease, cholesterol problems, alopecia, cancer, epilepsy, seizures, depression and anxiety. You'd be amazed at the number of people who stop taking drugs with her guidance. She helped thousands of clients over the past 5 years.

She is also an author of over 30 books from the 2 massive series: "Air Fryer Boot Camp" & "The Rules of Ketogenic Life", currently available!

Table of Contents

KETO DESSERT & CHAFFLE COOKBOOK 2021 WITH PICTURES

KETO BREAD MACHINE COOKBOOK 2021 WITH PICTURES

THE HEALTHY KETO MEAL PREP COOKBOOK WITH PICTURES

Keto Dessert & Chaffle Cookbook 2021 with Pictures

Quick and Easy, Sugar-Low Bombs, Chaffle and Cakes Recipes to Shed Weight, Boost Your Mood and Live Ketogenic lifestyle

By
Jamie Carter

Table of Contents

Introduction

The ketogenic diet or Keto is a low-carbohydrate, mild protein, high-fat diet that will help you lose fat more efficiently. It has several advantages for weight reduction, wellbeing, and efficiency, so a rising number of healthcare professionals & practitioners recommend it.

Fat as a form of nutrition

For nutrition, the body uses three fuel sources: carbohydrates, fats and proteins. Carbohydrates convert into blood sugar or glucose in the bloodstream and are the primary fuel source for the body. If carbohydrates are not accessible, your body then depends on fat as an energy source. Protein is the primary building block of muscles and tissues. Protein could also be processed into glucose in a pinch and utilized for energy.

The keto diet encourages your body to utilize fat as the primary source of nutrition instead of carbohydrates, a ketosis mechanism. You consume too little carbs on the keto diet that the body cannot depend on glucose for nutrition. And your body turns to utilize fat for energy rather than carbs, as keto foods are filled with fat. A major part of the calories, almost 70 to 80% come from fat, consuming 15 to 20% of calories from protein and barely 5% calories from carbohydrates (that makes for about 20 to 30 grams of carbohydrates per day, depending on the weight and height of a person).

Meal options in regular diets

To conquer the weight reduction fight, it becomes tough to continue the dieting combat for a long period. Many people revert to the previous eating patterns after only a few weeks when confronted with the difficulty and limited food ranges of many diets, especially vegan, low-fat and low-calorie diets. For starters, the ketogenic diet is incredibly beneficial for weight reduction, but following specific food choices can be overwhelming. Only after three weeks can you begin noticing significant effects; however, the complications and inconvenience of transitioning to an effective ketogenic diet may deter you from keeping to the program long enough to reap the benefits.

Thankfully, to render your keto diet ever more efficient, successful and simple to use, you will build an array of foods, preparing strategies, tips and suggestions. One hidden tool can be used from the diet's outset, without much details of the keto diet, which is continued even after achieving the weight loss target.

That hidden preferred weapon is the "Fat Bomb."

The Fat Bomb

The fat bombs in the keto diet play a major role in motivation for the dieters. Indulging in a high fat dessert gives you a stress-free environment to continue your diet. These fat bombs provide the correct amounts of fat, carbohydrates, and protein resulting in weight reduction while supplying the user with sustained energy. They do this by supplementing your diet with chemicals that hold your body in a fat-burning state, even after you have had a fulfilling meal.

The Keto diet aims to rely on foods that are high in fat and low in carbs. By modifying what the body utilizes as food, it helps facilitate weight reduction. Carbohydrates, like those present in sugars and bread, are usually transformed into energy. If the body cannot have enough nutrients, the body begins to burn fat as a substitute for energy.

Your liver converts the fat into ketones, which are a form of acid. Getting a certain amount of ketones in your body will lead you to a biochemical condition known as ketosis. Your body can burn stored fat for fuel; thus, you will losing weight when you go through ketosis.

To reach a ketosis condition, it takes between one to ten days of consuming a low-carb, high-fat diet; to sustain the fat-burning cycle of ketosis, you have to continue consuming the keto diet. Eating fatty foods will help you more easily get into ketosis and sustain it for longer periods.

Fat bombs are 90% fat, making them the ideal keto addition for beginners and lifetime keto adherents. They hold you in a ketosis state and can provide health advantages unlike many other high protein foods; you can snack on fat bombs or have them as dinners or as have as a side dish too. They are simple to produce and are available in a range of varieties, from sweet to savory.

Can Fat Bombs Be Healthy?

Ketogenic fat bombs are fueled by two major ingredients: high-fat dairy and coconut oil. Both of these components have several powerful health advantages. Coconut produces a form of fat known as MCTs (medium-chain triglycerides), which gives the body additional ketones that can be readily consumed and used to sustain ketosis.

There are distinct health advantages of consuming high-fat dairy fat bombs. High-fat dairy products produce fatty acids known as CLA (conjugated linoleic acid), minerals and vitamins. Data indicates that CLA plays a significant role in the body's breakdown of fat and may lower cardiac attack and stroke risk.

Eating high-fat dairy meals prior to bedtime may help burn fat when still sleeping. Fat burned while you sleep the body with an energy that does not need to metabolize stress hormones or depend on sugar.

Keto Diet and Mood

There are various comments from individuals on a keto diet that probably indicate the association between the keto diet and mood changes. Various hypotheses connect the keto diet to mood regulation, even if only partly.

The explanation of why the keto diet aids in accelerated weight reduction and reversal of multiple chronic weight-related problems lead people to come out of the despair of "I am not healthy." As a consequence of the results themselves, most people report a positive attitude by adopting a keto diet. But is that important? What makes a difference is that it has a positive and long-lasting effect. Some research also shows that a ketogenic diet may help combat depression since it provides anti-inflammatory benefits. Inflammations are associated with, at least certain, forms of depression. A few of the advantages are provided below that create the relationship between the keto diet and mood. A keto diet:

1. Helps regulate energy highs and lows.

Ketones offer an immediate energy supply for your brain since they are metabolized quicker than glucose. Ketones give a long-lasting, more accurate and reliable energy supply, and when your body understands it can access your fat reserves for food as well, the brain does not worry.

2. Neurogenesis improvement

Dietary consumption is a crucial element in assessing neurogenesis. A reduced degree of neurogenesis is correlated with multiple depressive illnesses. On the other side, a higher rate increases emotional endurance.

3. Reduces and Brings Down Inflammation

The Keto Diet provides healthy nutritional options, so you avoid consuming inflammatory and refined products. Consuming anti-inflammatory food can have a direct impact on the attitude. If you eat nutritious food high in protein, healthy fats and low-carb vegetables, it reduces inflammation.

4. Feeds the brain.

The good fat you consume on Keto fuels your brain and stabilizes your mood. As your brain is composed of 60% fat, it requires an excess of healthy fats to function properly.

So go ahead and try these easy to make lo carb hi fat desserts and lose weight deliciously!

Chapter 1- Low Carb Desserts

1. 10 Minutes Chocolate Mousse

Prep. Time: 10 minutes

Servings: 4

The serving size is ½ cup

Nutrition as per serving:

218 kcal / 23g fat / 5g carbs / 2g fiber / 2g protein = 3g net carbs

Ingredients

- Powdered sweetener 1/4 cup
- Cocoa powder, unsweetened, sifted 1/4 cup
- Vanilla extract 1tsp.
- Heavy whipping cream 1 cup
- Kosher salt 1/4tsp.

Directions

With an electric beater, beat the cream to form stiff peaks. Put in the sweetener, cocoa powder, salt, vanilla and whisk till all ingredients are well combined.

2. The Best Keto Cheesecake

Prep. Time: 20 minutes

Cook Time: 50 minutes

Setting Time: 8 hours

Servings: 12

The serving size is 1 slice

Nutrition as per serving:

600kcal / 54g fat / 7g carbs / 2g fiber / 14g protein = 5 g net carbs

Ingredients

Layer of crust

- Powdered sweetener 1/4 cup
- Almond flour 1 1/2 cups
- Butter melted 6 tbsp.
- Cinnamon 1tsp.

Filling

- Cream cheese, full fat, room temperature (8 oz.)
- Powdered Sweetener 2 Cups
- Eggs at room temperature 5 Large
- Sour cream at room temperature 8 Oz.
- Vanilla extract 1 Tbsp.

Directions

1. Heat the oven to 325F.
2. Arrange the rack in the center of the oven. Mix dry ingredients for the crust in a medium mixing bowl. Mix in the butter. Transfer the crust mixture into a springform pan (10-inch x 4- inch), and using your fingers, press halfway up and around the sides. Then press the mixture with a flat bottom cup into the pan. Chill the crust for about 20 minutes.
3. Beat the cream cheese (at room temperature) in a large mixing container, with an electric beater or a
4. Hand mixer until fluffy and light.

5. If using a stand mixer, attach the paddle accessory.
6. Add in about 1/3rd of sweetener at a time and beat well.
7. Add in one egg at a time beating until well incorporated.
8. Lastly, add in the sour cream, vanilla and mix until just combined.
9. Pour this cheesecake mixture onto the crust and smooth out the top. Place in the heated oven and examine after 50 minutes. The center should not jiggle, and the top should not be glossy anymore.
10. Turn the oven off and open the door slightly, leaving the cheesecake inside for about 30 minutes.
11. Take out the cheesecake and run a knife between the pan and the cheesecake (this is to unstick the cake but don't remove the springform yet). Leave for 1 hour.
12. Chill for at least 8 hrs. loosely covered with plastic wrap.
13. Take off the sides of the springform pan, decorate & serve.

Note: all the ingredients to make the cheesecake should be at room temperature. Anything refrigerated must be left out for at least 4 hrs.

3. Butter Pralines

Prep. Time: 5 minutes

Cook Time: 11 minutes

Chilling Time: 1 hour

Servings: 10

The serving size is 2 Butter Pralines

Nutrition as per serving:

338kcal / 36g fat / 3g carbs / 2g fiber / 2g protein = 1g net carbs

Ingredients

• Salted butter 2 Sticks
• Heavy Cream 2/3 Cup
• Granular Sweetener 2/3 Cup
• Xanthan gum ½ tsp.
• Chopped pecans 2 Cups
• Sea salt

Directions

1. Line parchment paper on a cookie sheet with or apply a silicone baking mat on it.
2. In a saucepan, brown the butter on medium-high heat, stirring regularly, for just about 5 minutes.
3. Add in the sweetener, heavy cream and xanthan gum. Stir and take off the heat.

4. Add in the nuts and chill to firm up, occasionally stirring, for about 1 hour. The mixture will become very thick. Shape into ten cookie forms and place on the lined baking sheet, and sprinkle with the sea salt, if preferred. Let chill until hardened.
5. Keep in a sealed container, keep refrigerated until serving.

4. Homemade Healthy Twix Bars

Prep. Time: 5 minutes

Cook Time: 20 minutes

Servings: 18 Bars

The serving size is 1 Bar

Nutrition as per serving:

111kcal / 7g fat / 8g carbs / 5g fiber / 4g protein = 3g net carbs

Ingredients

For the cookie layer

- Coconut flour 3/4 cup
- Almond flour 1 cup
- Keto maple syrup 1/4 cup
- Sweetener, granulated 1/2 cup
- Flourless keto cookies 1/4 cup
- Almond milk 1/2 cup

For the gooey caramel

- Cashew butter (or any seed or nut butter) 1 cup
- Sticky sweetener of choice 1 cup
- Coconut oil 1 cup
- For the chocolate coating
- Chocolate chips 2 cups

Directions

1. Line parchment paper in a loaf pan or square pan and set aside.
2. In a big mixing bowl, put in almond flour, coconut flour, and then granulated. Combine very well. Mix in the keto syrup and stir to make it into a thick dough.
3. Add the crushed keto cookies and also add a tbsp. of milk to keep it a thick batter. If the batter stays too thick, keep adding milk by tablespoon. Once desired consistency is achieved, shift the batter to the prepared pan and smooth it out. Chill.
4. Combine the cashew butter, coconut oil and syrup on the stovetop or a microwave-safe dish and heat until mixed. Beat very well to make sure the coconut oil is

completely mixed. Drizzle the caramel over the prepared cookie layer and shift to the freezer.

5. When the bars are hard, take out of the pan and slice into 18 bars. Once more, put it back in the freezer.

6. Liquefy the chocolate chips by heat. Using two forks, dip each Twix bar into the melted chocolate till evenly covered. Cover all the bars with chocolate. Chill until firm.

5. Best Chocolate Chip cookie

Prep. Time: 5 minutes

Cook Time: 20 minutes

Servings: 15 Cookies

The serving size is 1 Cookie

Nutrition as per serving:

98kcal / 6g fat / 12g carbs / 5g fiber / 5g protein = 7g net carbs

Ingredients

- Almond flour blanched 2 cups
- Baking powder 1 tsp
- Cornstarch 1/4 cup
- Coconut oil 2 tbsp.
- Sticky sweetener, keto-friendly 6 tbsp.
- Almond extract 1 tsp
- Coconut milk, unsweetened 1/4 cup
- Chocolate chips 1/2 cup

Directions

1. Heat oven up to 350F/175C. Line parchment paper on a large cookie tray and put it aside.

2. Place all the dry ingredients in a big mixing bowl, and combine well.

3. Melt the keto-friendly-sticky sweetener, almond extract and coconut oil in a microwave-safe proof or stovetop. Then mix it into the dry mixture, adding milk to combine very well. Stir through your chocolate chips.

4. Form small balls with slightly wet hands from the cookie dough. Set the balls up on the lined cookie tray. Then form them into cookies by pressing them with a fork. Bake for 12 to 15 minutes till they brown.

5. Take out from the oven, allowing to cool on the tray completely.

6. White Chocolate Dairy Free Peanut Butter Cups

Prep. Time: 5 minutes

Cook Time: 5 minutes

Servings: 40

The serving size is 1 cup

Nutrition as per serving:

117kcal / 6g fat / 14g carbs / 10g fiber / 3g protein = 4g net carbs

Ingredients

- White Chocolate Bar, Sugar-free, coarsely chopped 4 cups
- Peanut butter, smooth (or sunflower seed butter) 1 cup
- Coconut flour 2 tbsp.
- Unsweetened coconut milk 2 tbsp.+ more if needed

Directions

1. Line muffin liners in a standard muffin tin of 12 cups or mini muffin tin of 20 cups and put aside.
2. Removing ½ a cup of your white chocolate, melt the remaining 3 1/2 cups on the stovetop or in a microwave-safe dish, till silky and smooth. Quickly, pour the melted white chocolate equally amongst the prepared muffin cups, scrape down the sides to remove all. Once done, chill
3. Meanwhile, start making the peanut butter filling. Mix the flour and peanut butter well. Adding a tsp. of milk at a time brings to the desired texture.
4. Take the hardened white chocolate cups, then equally pour the peanut butter filling among all of them. After all, is used up, take white chocolate that was kept aside and melt them. Then pour it on each of the cups to cover fully. Chill until firm.

7. Chocolate Crunch Bars

Prep. Time: 5 minutes

Cook Time: 5 minutes

Servings: 20 servings

The serving size is 1 Bar

Nutrition as per serving:

155kcal / 12g fat / 4g carbs / 2g fiber / 7g protein = 2g net carbs

Ingredients

- Chocolate chips (stevia sweetened), 1 1/2 cups
- Almond butter (or any seed or nut butter) 1 cup
- Sticky sweetener (swerve sweetened or monk fruit syrup) 1/2 cup
- Coconut oil 1/4 cup
- Seeds and nuts (like almonds, pepitas, cashews, etc.) 3 cups

Directions

1. Line parchment paper on a baking dish of 8 x 8-inch and put it aside.
2. Combine the keto-friendly chocolate chips, coconut oil, almond butter and sticky sweetener and melt on a stovetop or a microwave-safe dish until combined.
3. Include nuts and seeds and combine until fully mixed. Pour this mixture into the parchment-lined baking dish smoothing it out with a spatula. Chill until firm.

Notes

Keep refrigerated

8. Easy Peanut Butter Cups

Prep. Time: 10minutes

Cook Time: 5minutes

Servings: 12

The serving size is 1 piece

Nutrition as per serving:

187kcal / 18g fat / 14g carbs / 11g fiber / 3g protein = 3g net carbs

Ingredients

Chocolate layers

- Dark chocolate(not bakers chocolate), Sugar-free, 10 oz. Divided
- Coconut oil 5 tbsp. (divided)
- Vanilla extracts 1/2 tsp. (divided) optional

Peanut butter layer

- Creamy Peanut butter 3 1/2 tbsp.
- Coconut oil 2 tsp.
- Powdered Erythritol (or to taste) 4 tsp.
- Peanut flour 1 1/2 tsp.
- Vanilla extracts 1/8 tsp. Optional
- Sea salt 1 pinch (or to taste) optional

Directions

1. Line parchment liners in a muffin pan
2. Prepare the chocolate layer on the stove, place a double boiler and heat half of the coconut oil and half of the chocolate, stirring regularly, until melted. (Alternatively use a microwave, heat for 20 seconds, stirring at intervals.). Add in half of the vanilla.
3. Fill each lined muffin cup with about 2 tsp. Of chocolate in each. Chill for around 10 minutes till the tops are firm.
4. Prepare the peanut butter filling: in a microwave or a double boiler, heat the coconut oil and peanut butter (similar to step 2). Mix in the peanut flour, powdered sweetener, sea salt and vanilla until smooth. Adjust salt and sweetener to taste if preferred.
5. Pour a tsp. Of the prepared peanut mixture into each cup with the chocolate layer. You don't want it to reach the edges. Chill for 10 minutes more till the tops are firm.
6. Now, prepare a chocolate layer for the top. Heat the leftover coconut oil and chocolate in a microwave or the double boiler (similar to step 2). Add in the vanilla.
7. Pour about 2 tsp of melted chocolate into each cup. It should cover the empty part and the peanut butter circles completely.
8. Again chill for at least 20 to 30 minutes, until completely solid. Keep in the refrigerator.

9. No-Bake Chocolate Coconut Bars

Prep. Time: 1 minute

Cook Time: 5 minutes

Servings: 12 bars

The serving size is 1 bar

Nutrition as per serving:

169 kcal / 17g fat / 5g carbs / 4g fiber / 2g protein = 1g net carbs

Ingredients

- Keto maple syrup 1/4 cup
- Coconut unsweetened, shredded 3 cups
- Coconut oil, melted 1 cup
- Lily's chocolate chips 1-2 cups

Directions

1. Line parchment paper in a large loaf pan or square pan and put aside.
2. Add all the ingredients to a large bowl and combine very well. Shift mixture to the prepared pan. Wet your hands lightly and press them into place. Chill for 30 minutes until firm. Cut into 12 bars.
3. Melt the sugar-free chocolate chips, and using two forks, dip each chilled bar into the melted chocolate and coat evenly. Evenly coat all the bars in the same way. Chill until chocolate solidifies.
4. Keep the Bars in a sealed container at room temperature. If you refrigerated or freeze them, thaw them completely before enjoying them.

10. Chocolate Peanut Butter Hearts

Prep. Time: 5 minutes

Cook Time: 5 minutes

Servings: 20 Hearts

The serving size is 1 Heart

Nutrition as per serving:

95kcal / 6g fat / 7g carbs / 5g fiber / 5g protein = 2g net carbs

Ingredients

- Smooth peanut butter 2 cups
- Sticky sweetener 3/4 cup

- Coconut flour 1 cup
- Chocolate chips of choice 1-2 cups

Directions

1. Line parchment paper on a large tray and put it aside.
2. Combine the keto-friendly sticky sweetener and peanut butter and melt on a stovetop or microwave-safe bowl until combined.
3. Include coconut flour and combine well. If the mixture is too thin, include more coconut flour. Leave for around 10 minutes to thicken.
4. Shape the peanut butter mixture into 18 to 20 small balls. Press each ball in. Then, using a heart-molded cookie cutter, shape the balls into hearts removing excess peanut butter mixture from the sides. Assemble the hearts on the lined tray and chill.
5. Melt the keto-friendly chocolate chips. With two forks, coat the chocolate by dipping each heart into it. Repeat with all hearts. When done, chill until firm.

Notes

Keep in a sealed jar at room temperature for up to 2 weeks, or refrigerate for up to 2 months.

11. Magic Cookies

Prep. Time: 10 minutes

Cook Time: 15 minutes

Servings: 15 cookies

The serving size is 1 cookie

Nutrition as per serving:

130kcal / 13g fat / 2g carbs / 1g fiber / 2g protein = 1g net carbs

Ingredients

- Butter softened 3 tbsp.
- Coconut oil 1/4 cup
- Granulated swerve sweetener 3 tbsp.
- Dark chocolate chips, sugar-free (like lily's) 1 cup
- Egg yolks 4 large
- Coconut flakes 1 cup
- Kosher salt 1/2 tsp.
- Walnuts roughly chopped 3/4 cup.

Directions

1. Heat oven up to 350° and line a parchment paper on a baking sheet. In a large mixing bowl, whisk together butter, coconut oil, sweetener, egg yolks and salt; stir in walnuts, coconut, and chocolate chips.
2. Drop spoonfuls of batter onto the prepared baking sheet. Place in the oven and bake for 15 mins until golden,

12. No-Bake Coconut Crack Bars

Prep. Time: 2 minutes

Cook Time: 3 minutes

Servings: 20

The serving size is 1 square

Nutrition as per serving:

108kcal / 11g fat / 2g carbs / 2g fiber /2g protein = 0g net carbs

Ingredients

- Coconut flakes unsweetened & Shredded 3 cups
- Coconut oil, melted 1 cup
- Maple syrup, monk fruit sweetened 1/4 cup (or any liquid sweetener of preference)

Directions

1. Line parchment paper on an 8 x 10-inch pan or an 8 x 8-inch pan and put aside. Or use a loaf pan.
2. Combine unsweetened shredded coconut, melted coconut oil, maple syrup (monk fruit sweetened) in a big mixing bowl and mix till you get a thick batter. If you find it crumbling, add a tsp. of water or a bit of extra syrup.
3. Transfer the coconut mixture to the lined pan. Press firmly with slightly wet hands into place. Chill until firmed. Cut into bars & enjoy!

13. Candied Pecans

Prep. Time: 5 minutes

Cook Time: 1 minute

Servings: 16 Servings

The serving size is 1 Serving

Nutrition as per serving:

139kcal / 15g fat / 3g carbs / 2g fiber / 2g protein = 1g net carbs

Ingredients

- Granulated sweetener divided 1 1/2 cups
- Vanilla extract 1 tsp
- Water 1/4 cup
- Cinnamon 1 tbsp.
- Raw pecans 3 cups

Directions

1. Over medium flame, heat a skillet or large pan.
2. Add 1 cup of the granulated sweetener, vanilla extract and water, and stir until fully mixed. Let it heat up, stirring in between.
3. Once the sweetener is fully melted, include your pecans. Stir around the pecans ensuring every nut is equally coated in the liquid mixture. Keep occasionally stirring till the sweetener starts to set on the pecans. Take off from the heat. Leave for 2 to 3 minutes.
4. Brea apart the pecans with a wooden spoon before they set together.
5. When cooled, mix with the granulated sweetener that was reserved earlier and cinnamon. Store in a sealed container.

14. Sugar-Free Flourless Cookies

Prep. Time: 2 minutes

Cook Time: 10 minutes

Servings: 14 cookies

The serving size is 1 Cookie

Nutrition as per serving:

101kcal / 9g fat / 3g carbs / 1g fiber / 5g protein = 3g net carbs

Ingredients

For the original style:

- Almond butter 1 cup
- Egg 1 large
- Granulated sweetener, stevia blend monk fruit, 3 /4 cup

For the egg-free style:

- Almond butter smooth 1 cup
- Chia seeds, ground 3-4 tbsp.
- Granulated sweetener, stevia blend monk fruit 3/4 cup

Directions

1. Heat the oven up to 350 degrees. Place parchment paper on a cookie sheet or a baking tray.
2. In a big mixing bowl, add all the ingredients and blend until well combined. When using the egg-free recipe, begin with 3 tbsps. of grounded chia seeds. Add an extra tbsp. if the mixture is still too thin.
3. Using your hands or a cookie scoop, shape small balls and place them 3 to 4 inches apart on the baking tray. Make into cookie shape by pressing down with a fork. Bake until cookies are beginning to get a golden brown color but still soft, or for 8 to 10 minutes. Take out from the oven, allowing to cool until firm but soft and chewy.

15. Salted Caramel Fudge

Prep. Time: 5 minutes

Cook Time: 5 minutes

Servings: 24 servings

The serving size is 1 fudge cup

Nutrition as per serving:

148kcal / 15g fat / 4g carbs / 2g fiber / 4g protein = 2g net carbs

Ingredients

- Cashew butter 2 cups
- Keto maple syrup 1/4 cup
- Coconut oil 1/2 cup

Directions

1. Line muffin liners in a mini muffin tin of 24-count and put aside.
2. Combine all the ingredients on a stovetop or in a microwave-safe dish and heat till melted.
3. Take off from heat and beat very well till a glossy, smooth texture remains.
4. Split the fudge mixture equally in the lined muffin tin. Chill for about 30 minutes, till firm.

16. Healthy Kit Kat Bars

Prep. Time: 5 minutes

Cook Time: 5 minutes

Servings: 20 Bars

The serving size is 1 Bar

Nutrition as per serving:

149kcal / 12g fat / 4g carbs / 2g fiber / 7g protein = 2g net carbs

Ingredients

- Keto granola 2 cups
- Almond butter (or any seed or nut butter) 1 cup
- Mixed seeds 1/2 cup
- Coconut oil 1/4 cup
- Mixed nuts 1/2 cup
- Dark chocolate chips, 1 1/2 cups
- Sticky sweetener 1/2 cup

Directions

1. Mix the mixed nuts, keto granola, and seeds in a big bowl. Put aside.
2. Melt the keto chocolate chips on the stovetop or in a microwave-safe dish. Include almond butter, coconut oil, and sticky sweetener. Heat until well combined.
3. Add the melted chocolate mixture onto the dry and combine until fully unified.
4. Shift the kit kat mixture to a pan of 10 x 10-inch lined with parchment. With a spatula, smooth out to a uniform layer. Chill for about 30 minutes, then slice into bars.

Notes: keep refrigerated

17. Healthy No-Bake Keto Cookie Bars

Prep. Time: 5 minutes

Cook Time: 25 minutes

Servings: 12 servings

The serving size is 1 Bar

Nutrition as per serving:

149kcal / 5g fat / 10g carbs / 6g fiber / 10g protein = 4g net carbs

Ingredients

For the cookie

- Almond flour blanched 1 1/2 cups
- Coconut flour 1/4 cup
- Cinnamon, a pinch
- Protein powder, vanilla flavor (optional) 2 scoops
- Granulated sweetener (like
- Sticky sweetener, keto-friendly, 1/2 cup
- Monk fruit sweetener) 2 tbsp.
- Vanilla extract 1/2 tsp
- Cashew butter (or any nut butter) 1/2 cup
- Sticky sweetener, keto-friendly, 1/2 cup
- Almond milk 1 tbsp.

For the protein icing

- Protein powder,
- Vanilla flavor 3 scoops
- Granulated sweetener, keto-friendly 1-2 tbsp. + for sprinkling 1/2 tsp
- Almond milk, (for batter) 1 tbsp.

For the coconut butter icing

- Coconut butter melted 4-6 tbsp.
- Sticky sweetener, 2 tbsp.
- Almond milk 1 tbsp.

Directions

1. Preparing sugar cookie base
2. Place tin foil in a baking pan of 8 x 8 inches and put aside.
3. Mix the protein powder, flours, granulated sweetener and cinnamon in a big mixing bowl, and put aside.
4. Melt the sticky sweetener with cashew butter on a stovetop or a microwave-proof bowl. Stir in the vanilla extract and add to the dry mixture. Beat superbly until fully combined. If the batter formed is too thick, add a tablespoon of almond milk with a tablespoon and mix well until desired consistency.

5. Pour the batter into the lined baking sheet and press tightly in place. Scatter the ½ teaspoon of keto-friendly granulated sweetener and chill for about 15 minutes until they are firm. Then add an icing of choice and chill for 30 minutes more to settle the icing before slicing.
6. Preparing the icing(s)
7. Mix all ingredients of the icings (separately) and, using almond milk, thin down the mixture till a very thick icing is formed.

18. Keto Chocolate Bark with Almonds and Bacon

Prep. Time: 30 minutes

Servings: 8 servings

The serving size is 1/8 of the recipe

Nutrition as per serving:

157kcal / 12.8g fat / 4g protein / 7.5g fiber / 12.7g carbs = 5.2g net carbs

Ingredients

- Sugar-free Chocolate Chips 1 bag (9 oz.)
- Chopped Almonds 1/2 cup
- Bacon cooked & crumbled2 slices

Directions

1. In a microwave-safe bowl, melt the chocolate chips on high in 30 seconds intervals, stirring every time until all chocolate is melted.
2. Include the chopped almonds into the melted chocolate and mix.
3. Line a baking sheet with parchment and pour the chocolate mixture on it in a thin layer of about 1/2 inch.
4. Immediately top the chocolate with the crumbled bacon and press in with a flat spoon.
5. Chill for around 20 minutes or till the chocolate has solidified. Peel the parchment away from the hardened chocolate and crack it into eight pieces. Keep refrigerated.

Chapter 2- Chaffles

1. Basic chaffle recipe

Prep. Time: 5 minutes

Cook Time: 5 minutes

Servings: 1 chaffle

The serving size is 1 chaffle

Nutrition as per serving:

291kcal / 23g fat / 1g carbs / 0g fiber / 20g protein = 1g net carbs

Ingredients

- Sharp cheddar cheese shredded 1/2 cup
- Eggs 1

Directions

1. Whisk the egg.
2. In the waffle maker, assemble 1/4 cup of shredded cheese.
3. Top the cheese with beaten egg.
4. Top with the remainder 1/4 cup of cheese.
5. Cook till it's golden and crispy. It will get crispier as it cools.

2. Keto Oreo Chaffles

Prep. Time: 15 minutes

Cook Time: 8 minutes

Servings: 2 full-size chaffles or 4 mini chaffles

The serving size is 2 chaffles

Nutrition as per serving:

381kcal / 14.6g fat / 14g carbs / 5g fiber / 17g protein = 9g net carbs

Ingredients

- Sugar-Free Chocolate Chips 1/2 cup
- Butter 1/2 cup
- Eggs 3
- Truvia 1/4 cup
- Vanilla extract 1tsp.
- For Cream Cheese Frosting
- Butter, room temperature 4 oz.
- Cream Cheese, room temperature 4 oz.
- Powdered Swerve 1/2 cup
- Heavy Whipping Cream 1/4 cup
- Vanilla extract 1tsp.

Directions

1. Melt the butter and chocolate for around 1 minute in a microwave-proof dish. Stir well. You really ought to use the warmth within the chocolate and butter to melt most of the clumps. You have overheated the chocolate; when you microwave, and all is melted, it means you have overheated the chocolate. So grab yourself a spoon and begin stirring. If required, add 10 seconds, but stir just before you plan to do so.
2. Put the eggs, vanilla and sweetener, in a bowl and whisk until fluffy and light.
3. In a steady stream, add the melted chocolate into the egg mix and whisk again until well-combined.
4. In a Waffle Maker, pour around 1/4 of the mixture and cook for 7 to-8 minutes until it's crispy.
5. Prepare the frosting as they are cooking.
6. Put all the frosting ingredients into a food processor bowl and mix until fluffy and smooth. To achieve the right consistency, include a little extra cream.
7. To create your Oreo Chaffle, spread or pipe the frosting evenly in between the two chaffles.
8. The waffle machine, do not overfill it! It will create a giant mess and ruin the batter and the maker, utilizing no more than 1/4 cup of the batter.

9. Leave the waffles to cool down a bit before frosting. It is going to help them to remain crisp.

10. To make the frosting, use room-temp butter and cream cheese.

3. Glazed Donut Chaffle

Prep. Time: 10 mins

Cook Time: 5 mins

Servings: 3 chaffles

The serving size is 1 chaffle

Nutrition as per serving:

312kcal / 15g fat / 6g carbs / 1g fiber / 9g protein = 5g net carbs

Ingredients

For the chaffles

- Mozzarella cheese shredded ½ cup
- Whey protein isolates Unflavored 2 tbsp.
- Cream Cheese 1 oz.
- Swerve confectioners (Sugar substitute) 2 tbsp.
- Vanilla extract ½tsp.
- Egg 1
- Baking powder ½tsp.

For the glaze topping:

- Heavy whipping cream2 tbsp.
- Swerve confectioners (sugar substitute) 3-4 tbsp.
- Vanilla extract ½tsp.

Directions

1. Turn on the waffle maker.
2. In a microwave-proof bowl, combine the cream cheese and mozzarella cheese. Microwave at 30-second breaks until it is all melted and stir to combine completely.
3. Include the whey protein, baking powder, 2 tbsp. Keto sweetener to the melted cheese, and work with your hands to knead until well combined.
4. Put the dough in a mixing bowl, and whisk in the vanilla and egg into it to form a smooth batter.
5. Put 1/3 of the mixture into the waffle machine, and let it cook for 3 to 5 minutes.
6. Repeat the above step 5 to make a total of three chaffles.

7. Whisk the glaze topping ingredients together and drizzle on top of the chaffles generously before serving.

4. Keto Pumpkin Chaffles

Prep. Time: 2 mins

Cook Time: 5 mins

Servings: 2 chaffles

The serving size is 2 chaffles

Nutrition as per serving: (without toppings)

250kcal / 15g fat / 5g carbs / 1g fiber / 23g protein = 4g net carbs

Ingredients

- Mozzarella cheese, shredded ½ cup
- Egg, beaten 1 whole
- Pumpkin purée 1 ½ tbsp.
- Swerve confectioners ½tsp.
- Vanilla extract ½tsp.
- Pumpkin pie spice ¼tsp.
- Pure maple extract ⅛tsp.
- For topping- optional
- roasted pecans, cinnamon, whip cream and sugar-free maple syrup

Directions

1. Switch on the Waffle Maker and begin preparing the mixture.
2. Add all the given ingredients to a bowl, except for the mozzarella cheese, and whisk. Include the cheese and combine until well mixed.
3. Grease the waffle plates and put half the mixture into the middle of the plate. Cover the lid for 4- to 6 minutes, based on how crispy Chaffles you like.
4. Take it out and cook the second one. Serve with all or some mix of toppings, like sugar-free maple syrup, butter, roasted pecans, and a dollop of whipping cream or ground cinnamon dust.

5. Cream Cheese Chaffle with Lemon Curd

Prep. Time: 5 minutes

Cook Time: 4 minutes

Additional Time: 40 minute

Servings: 2-3 serving

The serving size is 1 chaffle

Nutrition as per serving:

302 kcals / 24g fat / 6g carbs / 1g fiber / 15g protein = 5g net carbs

Ingredients

- One batch keto lemon curd (recipe here)
- Eggs 3 large
- Cream cheese softened 4 oz.
- Lakanto monkfruit (or any low carb sweetener) 1 tbsp.
- Vanilla extract 1tsp.
- Mozzarella cheese shredded 3/4 cup
- Coconut flour 3 tbsp.
- Baking powder 1tsp.
- Salt 1/3tsp.
- Homemade keto whipped cream (optional) (recipe here)

Directions

1. Prepare lemon curd according to Directions and let cool in the refrigerator.
2. Turn on the waffle maker and grease it with oil.
3. Take a small bowl, put coconut flour, salt and baking powder. Combine and put aside.
4. Take a large bowl, put cream cheese, eggs, vanilla and sweetener. With an electric beater, beat until foamy. You may see chunks of cream cheese, and that is okay.

5. Include mozzarella cheese into the egg mixture and keep beating.
6. Pour the dry ingredients into the egg mixture and keep mixing until well blended.
7. Put batter into the preheated waffle machine and cook.
8. Take off from waffle machine; spread cooled lemon curd, top with keto whipped cream and enjoy.

6. Strawberries & Cream Keto Chaffles

Prep. Time: 25 minutes

Cook Time: 10 minutes

Servings: 8 chaffles

The serving size is 1 chaffle

Nutrition as per serving:

328cals / 12g fat / 8g carbs / 4g fiber /6g protein = 4g net carbs

Ingredients

- Cream cheese 3 oz.
- Mozzarella cheese, shredded 2 cups
- Eggs, beaten 2
- Almond flour 1/2 cup
- Swerve confectioner sweetener 3 tbsp. + 1 tbsp.
- Baking powder 2tsps
- Strawberries 8
- Whipped cream 1 cup (canister - 2 tbsp. Per waffle)

Directions

1. In a microwavable dish, add the mozzarella and cream cheese, cook for 1 minute, mixing well. If the cheese is all melted, then go to the next step. Else cook for another 30 seconds stirring well.
2. Take another bowl, whisk eggs, including the almond flour, 3 tbsp. of keto sweetener, and baking powder.
3. Include the melted cheese mixture into the egg and almond flour mixture and combine well. Carefully add in 2 strawberries coarsely chopped. Chill for 20 minutes.
4. Meanwhile, slice the unused strawberries and mix with 1 tbsp. of Swerve. Chill.
5. Take out the batter from the refrigerator after 20 minutes. Heat the waffle iron and grease it.
6. Put 1/4 cup of the batter in the mid of the heated waffle iron. Ensuring the waffles are small makes it easier to remove from the waffle maker.

7. Transfer to a plate when cooked and cool before adding whipped cream and topping with strawberries.

This recipe gave me eight small waffles.

7. Keto Peanut Butter Cup Chaffle

Prep. Time: 2 minutes

Cook Time: 5 minutes

Servings: 2 Chaffles

The serving size is 1 chaffle + filling

Nutrition as per serving:

264kcal / 21.6g fat / 7.2g carbs / 2g fiber / 9.45g protein = 4.2g net carbs

Ingredients

For the Chaffle

- Heavy Cream 1 tbsp.
- Vanilla Extract 1/2 tsp
- Egg 1
- Cake Batter Flavor 1/2 tsp
- Unsweetened Cocoa 1 tbsp.
- Coconut Flour 1 tsp
- Lakanto Powdered Sweetener 1 tbsp.
- Baking Powder 1/4 tsp

For Peanut Butter Filling

- Heavy Cream 2 tbsp.
- All-natural Peanut Butter 3 tbsp.
- Lakanto Powdered Sweetener 2 tsp

Directions

1. Preheat a waffle maker.
2. Combine all the chaffle ingredients in a small mixing bowl.
3. Put half of the chaffle batter into the middle of the waffle machine and cook for 3 to 5 minutes.
4. Cautiously remove and duplicate for the second chaffle. Leave chaffles for a couple of minutes to let them crisp up.
5. Prepare the peanut butter filling by blending all the ingredients together and layer between chaffles.

8. Vanilla Chocolate Chip

Prep. Time: 1 minute

Cook Time: 4 minutes

Servings: 1 serving

The serving size is 1 large or 2 mini chaffle

Nutrition as per serving:

297.6 kcal. / 20.1g fat / 5.2g carbs / 1.5g fiber / 22.2g protein = 3.9g net carbs

Ingredients

- Mozzarella shredded 1/2 cup
- Eggs 1 medium
- Granulated sweetener keto 1 tbsp.
- Vanilla extract 1 tsp
- Almond meal or flour 2 tbsp.
- Chocolate chips, sugar-free 1 tbsp.

Directions

1. Mix all the ingredients in a large bowl.
2. Turn on the waffle maker. When it is heated, grease with olive oil and put half the mixture into the waffle machine. Cook for 2 to 4 minutes, then take out and repeat. It will make 2 small-chaffles per recipe.
3. Enjoy with your favorite toppings.

9. Chaffle Churro

Prep. Time: 10 minutes

Cook Time: 6-10 minutes

Servings: 2

The serving size is 4 churros

Nutrition as per serving:

189 kcals / 14.3g fat / 5.g carbs / 1g fiber / 10g protein = 4g net carbs

Ingredients

- Egg 1
- Almond flour 1 Tbsp.
- Vanilla extract ½ tsp.
- Cinnamon divided 1 tsp.

- Baking powder ¼ tsp.
- Shredded mozzarella ½ cup.
- Swerve confectioners (or any sugar substitute) 1 Tbsp.
- Swerve brown sugar (keto-friendly sugar substitute) 1 Tbsp.
- Butter melted 1 Tbsp.

Directions

1. Heat the waffle iron.
2. Combine the almond flour, egg, vanilla extract, baking powder, ½ tsp of cinnamon, swerve confectioners' sugar and shredded mozzarella in a bowl, and stir to combine well.
3. Spread half of the batter equally onto the waffle iron, and let it cook for 3 to 5 minutes. Cooking for more time will give a crispier chaffle.
4. Take out the cooked chaffle and pour the remaining batter onto it. Close the lid and cook for about 3 to 5 minutes.
5. Make both the chaffles into strips.
6. Put the cut strips in a bowl and drizzle on melted butter generously.
7. In another bowl, stir together the keto brown sugar and the leftover ½ tsp of cinnamon until well-combined.
8. Toss the churro chaffle strips in the sugar-cinnamon mixture in the bowl to coat them evenly.

10. Keto Cauliflower Chaffles Recipe

Prep. Time: 5 minutes

Cook Time: 4 minutes

Servings: 2 chaffles

The serving size is 2 chaffles

Nutrition as per serving:

246kcal / 16g fat / 7g carbs / 2g fiber / 20g protein = 5g net carbs

Ingredients

- Riced cauliflower 1 cup
- Garlic powder 1/4tsp.
- Ground black pepper 1/4tsp.
- Italian seasoning 1/2tsp.
- Kosher salt 1/4tsp.
- Mozzarella cheese shredded 1/2 cup
- Eggs 1

- Parmesan cheese shredded 1/2 cup

Directions

1. In a blender, add all the ingredients and blend well. Turn the waffle maker on.
2. Put 1/8 cup of parmesan cheese onto the waffle machine. Ensure to cover up the bottom of the waffle machine entirely.
3. Cover the cheese with the cauliflower batter, then sprinkle another layer of parmesan cheese on the cauliflower mixture. Cover and cook.
4. Cook for 4 to 5 minutes, or till crispy.
5. Will make 2 regular-size chaffles or 4 mini chaffles.
6. It freezes well. Prepare a big lot and freeze for the future.

11. Zucchini Chaffles

Prep. Time: 10 minutes

Cook Time: 5 minutes

Servings: 2 chaffles

The serving size is 1 chaffle

Nutrition as per serving:

194kcal / 13g fat / 4g carbs / 1g fiber / 16g protein = 3g net carbs

Ingredients

- Zucchini, grated 1 cup
- Eggs, beaten 1

- Parmesan cheese shredded 1/2 cup
- Mozzarella cheese shredded 1/4 cup
- Dried basil, 1tsp. Or fresh basil, chopped 1/4 cup
- Kosher Salt, divided 3/4tsp.
- Ground Black Pepper 1/2tsp.

Directions

1. Put the shredded zucchini in a bowl and Sprinkle salt, about 1/4tsp on it and leave it aside to gather other ingredients. Moments before using put the zucchini in a paper towel, wrap and press to wring out all the extra water.
2. Take a bowl and whisk in the egg. Include the mozzarella, grated zucchini, basil, and pepper 1/2tsp of salt.
3. Cover the waffle maker base with a layer of 1 to 2 tbsp. of the shredded parmesan.
4. Then spread 1/4 of the zucchini batter. Spread another layer of 1 to 2 tbsp. of shredded parmesan and shut the lid.
5. Let it cook for 4 to 8 minutes. It depends on the dimensions of your waffle machine. Normally, once the chaffle is not emitting vapors of steam, it is nearly done. For the greatest results, let it cook until good and browned.
6. Take out and duplicate for the next waffle.

Will make 4 small chaffles or 2 full-size chaffles in a Mini waffle maker.

12. Keto Pizza Chaffle

Prep. Time: 10 minutes

Cook Time: 30 minutes

Servings: 2 servings

The serving size is 1 chaffle

Nutrition as per serving:

76 kcal / 4.3g fat / 4.1g carbs / 1.2g fiber / 5.5g protein = 3.2g net carbs

Ingredients

- Egg 1
- Mozzarella cheese shredded 1/2 cup
- Italian seasoning a pinch
- Pizza sauce No sugar added 1 tbsp.
- Toppings – pepperoni, shredded cheese (or any other toppings)

Directions

- Heat the waffle maker.
- Whisk the egg, and Italian seasonings in a small mixing bowl, together.
- Stir in the cheese, leaving a few tsps. for layering.
- Layer a tsp of grated cheese onto the preheated waffle machine and allow it to cook for about 30 seconds.
- It will make a crispier crust.
- Pour half the pizza mixture into the waffle maker and allow to cook for around 4 minutes till it's slightly crispy and golden brown!
- Take out the waffle and make the second chaffle with the remaining mixture.
- Spread the pizza sauce, pepperoni and shredded cheese. Place in Microwave and heat on high for around 20 seconds and done! On the spot Chaffle PIZZA!

13. Crispy Taco Chaffle Shells

Prep. Time: 5 minutes

Cook Time: 8 minutes

Servings: 2 chaffles

The serving size is 1 chaffle

Nutrition as per serving:

258kcal / 19g fat / 4g carbs / 2g fiber / 18g protein = 2g net carbs

Ingredients

- Egg white 1
- Monterey jack cheese shredded 1/4 cup
- Sharp cheddar cheese shredded 1/4 cup
- Water 3/4 tsp
- Coconut flour 1 tsp
- Baking powder 1/4 tsp
- Chili powder 1/8 tsp
- Salt a pinch

Directions

1. Turn on the Waffle iron and lightly grease it with oil when it is hot.
2. In a mixing bowl, mix all of the above ingredients and blend to combine.
3. Pour half of the mixture onto the waffle iron and shut the lid. Cook for 4 minutes without lifting the lid. The chaffle will not set in less than 4 minutes.
4. Take out the cooked taco chaffle and put it aside. Do the same process with the remaining chaffle batter.

5. Put a muffin pan upside down and assemble the taco chaffle upon the cups to make into a taco shell. Put aside for a few minutes.

6. When it is firm, fill it with your favorite Taco Meat fillings. Serve.

Enjoy this delicious keto crispy taco chaffle shell with your favorite toppings.

Chapter 3- Keto Cakes and Cupcakes

1. Chocolate Cake with Chocolate Icing

Prep. Time: 10 minutes

Cook Time: 25 minutes

Servings: 9 slices

The serving size is 1 slice

Nutrition as per serving:

358kcal / 33g fat / 11g carbs / 6g fiber / 8g protein = 5g net carbs

Ingredients

- Coconut flour 3/4 cup
- Granular sweetener 3/4 cup
- Cocoa powder 1/2 cup
- Baking powder 2tsps
- Eggs 6
- Heavy whipping cream 2/3 cup
- Melted butter 1/2 cup

- For chocolate icing
- Heavy whipping cream 1 cup
- Keto granular sweetener 1/4 cup
- Vanilla extracts 1tsp.
- Cocoa powder sifted 1/3 cup

Directions

1. Heat the oven up to 350F.
2. Oil a cake pan of 8x8.
3. In a large mixing bowl, put all the cake ingredients to blend well with an electric mixer or a stand mixer.
4. Transfer the batter to the oiled pan and put in the heated oven for 25 minutes or till a toothpick inserted in the center comes out clean.
5. Take out from the oven. Leave to cool fully before icing.
6. Prepare the Icing
7. With an electric mixer, beat the whipping cream until stiff peaks form. Include the cocoa powder, swerve, and vanilla. Keep beating until just combined.
8. Spread the icing evenly all over the cake and serve. Keep any remains in the refrigerator.

2. 4 Ingredients Cheesecake Fluff

Prep. Time: 10 minutes

Servings: 6

The serving size is ½ cup

Nutrition as per serving:

258kcal / 27g fat / 4g carbs / 0g fiber / 4g protein = 4g net carbs

Ingredients

- Heavy Whipping Cream1 Cup
- Cream Cheese, Softened 1 Brick (8 oz.)
- Lemon Zest 1 tsp.
- Keto-friendly Granular Sweetener 1/2 Cup

Directions

1. Prepare the Fluff
2. Put the heavy cream in a bowl of a stand mixer and beat until stiff peaks begin to form. An electric beater or a hand beater can also be used.
3. Transfer the whipped cream into a separate bowl and put aside

4. To the same stand mixer bowl, add the cream cheese (softened), sweetener, zest, and whisk until smooth.
5. Now add the whipped cream to the cream cheese into the mixer bowl. Fold with a spatula gently till it is halfway combined. Finish whipping with the stand mixer until smooth.
6. Top with your fave toppings and serve.

3. Mug Cake Peanut Butter, Chocolate or Vanilla

Prep. Time: 4 minutes

Cook Time: 1 minute

Servings: 1

The serving size is 1 mug cake

Nutrition as per serving:

(For mug cake with almond flour: chocolate flavor and no chocolate chips)

312 kcal / 7 carbs/ 28g fat / 12g protein/4g fiber = 3 net carbs

(Peanut butter flavor and no chocolate chips)

395 kcal / 8 carbs /35g fat / 15g protein/4g fiber = 5 net carb

(Vanilla flavor and no chocolate chips)

303 kcal / 5 carbs/ 28g fat / 11g protein /2g fiber = 3 net carb

Ingredients

- Butter melted 1 Tbsp.
- Almond flour 3 Tbsp. or Coconut flour 1 Tbsp.
- Granular Sweetener 2 Tbsp.
- Sugar-free Peanut butter 1 Tbsp. (For Peanut Butter flavor)
- Cocoa powder 1 Tbsp. (For Chocolate flavor)
- Baking powder ½ tsp.
- Egg, beaten 1
- Sugar-free Chocolate Chips 1 Tbsp.
- Vanilla few drops

Directions

For Vanilla flavor

1. In a microwave-proof coffee mug, heat the butter for 10 seconds to melt in the microwave.
2. Include the almond flour or coconut flour, baking powder, sweetener, beaten egg and vanilla. Combine well.
3. For 60 seconds, microwave on high, ensuring not to overcook; otherwise, it will come out dry. Sprinkle keto chocolate chips on top if preferred or stir in before cooking.

For Chocolate flavor

In a microwave-proof coffee mug, heat the butter for 10 seconds to melt in the microwave. Include the almond flour or coconut flour, cocoa powder, sweetener, baking powder, beaten egg and vanilla. Combine well. For 60 seconds, microwave on high, ensuring not to overcook; it will come out dry. Sprinkle keto chocolate chips on top if preferred.

For Peanut Butter flavor

1. In a microwave-proof coffee mug, heat the butter for 10 seconds to melt in the microwave.
2. Include the almond flour or coconut flour, baking powder, sweetener, beaten egg and vanilla. Combine well. Stir in peanut butter. For 60 seconds, microwave on high, ensuring not to overcook; otherwise, it will come out dry. Sprinkle keto chocolate chips on top if preferred.

Directions for Baking: Bake in an oven-safe small bowl. Bake in the oven for 15 to 20 minutes at 350.

4. Chocolate Coconut Flour Cupcakes

Prep. Time: 10 minutes

Cook Time: 25 minutes

Servings: 12 cupcakes

The serving size is 1 cupcake

Nutrition as per serving:

268 kcal / 22g fat / 6g carbs / 3g fiber / 6g protein = 3g net carbs

Ingredients

For Cupcakes:

- Butter melted 1/2 cup
- Cocoa powder 7 tbsp.
- Instant coffee granules 1 tsp (optional)
- Eggs at room temperature 7
- Vanilla extracts 1 tsp
- Coconut flour 2/3 cup
- Baking powder 2 tsp
- Swerve sweetener 2/3 cup
- Salt 1/2 tsp
- Hemp milk or unsweetened almond milk 1/2 cup (+more)

For Espresso Buttercream:

- Hot water 2 tbsp.
- Instant coffee or instant espresso powder 2 tsp
- Whipping cream 1/2 cup
- Butter softened 6 tbsp.
- Cream cheese softened 4 oz.
- Swerve powdered sweetener 1/2 cup

Directions

For Cupcakes:

1. Heat the oven up to 350F and line silicone liners or parchment on a muffin tin.
2. Mix together the cocoa powder, melted butter, and espresso powder in a large mixing bowl,
3. Include the vanilla and eggs and whisk until well combined. Now add in the coconut flour, baking powder, salt and sweetener, and mix until smooth.
4. Pour the almond milk in and stir. If the batter is very thick, add in 1 tbsp. of almond milk at a time to thin it out. It should not be pourable but of scoopable consistency.
5. Scoop the batter equally among the prepared muffin tins and put in the oven's center rack, baking for 20-25 minutes. Check the cupcakes with a tester inserted into the center comes out clean, then cupcakes are done. Leave to cool in the pan for 5 to 10 minutes, and then cool completely on a wire rack.

For Buttercream:

1. Dissolve the coffee in hot water. Put aside.
2. Whip cream using an electric mixer until stiff peaks are formed. Put aside.
3. Beat cream cheese, butter, and sweetener all together in a medium mixing bowl until creamy. Include coffee mixture and mix until combined. fold in the whipped cream Using a rubber spatula carefully till well combined.
4. Layer frosting on the cooled cupcakes with an offset spatula or a knife.

5. Low-carb red velvet cupcakes/ cake

Prep. Time: 15-30 minutes

Cook Time: 20-25 minutes

Servings: 12 slice

The serving size is 1 slice

Nutrition as per serving:

193kcals / 12g fat / 6.4g carbs / 1g fiber / 5.9g protein = 5.4g net carbs

Ingredients

- Almond flour 1+ 3/4 cups
- Swerve confectioner sweetener (not substitutes) 2/3 cup
- Cocoa powder 2 tbsp.
- Baking powder 2tsp.
- Baking soda 1/2tsp.
- Eggs 2
- Full fat coconut milk 1/2 cup + 2 tbsp.
- Olive oil 3 tbsp.
- Apple cider vinegar 1 tbsp.
- Vanilla extract 1 tbsp.
- Red food coloring 2 tbsp.

For frosting

- Cream cheese at room temperature 1 container (8 oz.)
- Butter softened 2 ½ tbsp.
- Swerve confectioner sweetener 1 cup
- Coconut milk 2 ½ tbsp.
- Vanilla extract 1tsp.
- Salt 1/8tsp.

**Double Frosting for Layer Cake

Directions

1. Preheat oven to 350 degrees
2. In a large mixing bowl, add the wet ingredients, eggs, milk, vanilla extract, olive oil, apple cider vinegar and food coloring. Blend until smooth.
3. Now sift together the cocoa powder, Swerve Confectioner, baking powder and baking soda, add to the wet ingredients, and incorporate it into the batter with an electric mixer or a hand whisk.
4. Lastly, sift in the almond flour. Moving the flour back and forth with a whisk will speed up the process significantly. Fold the sifted flour gently into the batter till smooth and all is well incorporated. Use the batter immediately.
5. To make Cupcakes: Scoop batter into the muffin liners, fill only up to 2/3 of liner -do not over-fill. Ensure the oven is heated, put in the oven for 15 minutes at 350 degrees, and then turn the muffin tin in 180 degrees and cook for an extra 10 minutes. (Bear in mind, oven times vary occasionally - humidity and altitude can impact things, so watch closely as they may need a few minutes more or even less).
6. Take out from the oven, do not remove from pan and set aside to cool completely.
7. For Layer Cake: 2 Layer- line parchment paper in two cake pans (8 inches each) and oil the sides. Transfer batter to both pans evenly. Use a wet spatula to spread the batter smoothly. Apply the same process for three layers, but using thinner pans as dividing the batter three ways-every layers will become thin.
8. Place pans into oven for 20-25 minutes baking at 350 degrees. Cautiously turn the pans 180 degrees halfway through baking and cover lightly with a foil. At 20 to 25 minutes, take out the pans; they will be a bit soft. Set them aside to cool completely. When they are cool, take a knife and run it around the side of the pan and turn them over carefully onto a plate or cooling rack and leave them for an extra 5 to 10 minutes before icing.
9. Meanwhile, prepare. Blend the softened butter and cream cheese together With an electric beater. Include milk and vanilla extract and beat again. Lastly, sift in the Swerve, salt mixing well one last time. If you want a thicker frosting, chill it in the refrigerator. Or adding more Swerve will give a thicker texture or add more milk to make it thinner. * For a layer cake, double the frosting recipe.
10. Spread or pipe frosting onto cupcakes, sprinkle some decoration if desired and enjoy!! To frost layer cake, it is simpler to first chill the layers in the freezer. Then frost and pile each layer to end frost the sides and top.

11. Keep any leftovers in a sealed box and refrigerate. Enjoy!

6. Vanilla Cupcakes

Prep. Time: 5 minutes

Cook Time: 20 minutes

Servings: 10 Cupcakes

The serving size is 1 cupcake

Nutrition as per serving:

153kcal / 13g fat / 4g carbs / 2g fiber / 5g protein = 2g net carbs

Ingredients

- Butter 1/2 cup
- Keto granulated sweetener 2/3 cup
- Vanilla extract 2 tsp
- Eggs whisked * See notes 6 large
- Milk of choice ** See notes 2 tbsp.
- Coconut flour 1/2 cup
- Baking powder 1 tsp
- Keto vanilla frosting 1 batch

Directions

1. Heat the oven up to 350F/180C. Place muffin liners in a 12-cup muffin tin and oil 10 of them.
2. Beat the butter, salt, sugar, eggs and vanilla extract together in a big mixing bowl when combined-well include the milk and mix until blended.
3. In another bowl, sift the baking powder and coconut flour together. Add the wet ingredients to the dry and mix until combined.

4. Pour the batter equally into the ten muffin cups, filling up to ¾ full. Place the cupcakes on the middle rack and bake for 17 to 20 minutes until the muffin top springs back to touch

5. Remove the muffin pan from the oven, set it aside to cool for 10 minutes, and then cool completely on a wire rack. Frost, when cooled.

7. Healthy Flourless Fudge Brownies

Prep. Time: 5 minutes

Cook Time: 20 minutes

Servings: 12 servings

The serving size is 1 Brownie

Nutrition as per serving:

86kcal / 5g fat / 5g carbs / 3g fiber / 7g protein = 2g net carbs

Ingredients

- Pumpkin puree 2 cups
- Almond butter 1 cup
- Cocoa powder 1/2 cup
- Granulated sweetener (or liquid stevia drops) 1/4 cup

For the Chocolate Coconut Frosting

- Chocolate chips 2 cups
- Coconut milk canned 1 cup
- For the chocolate protein frosting
- Protein powder, chocolate flavor 2 scoops
- Granulated sweetener 1-2 tbsp.
- Seed or nut butter of choice 1-2 tbsp.
- Milk or liquid *1 tbsp.

For the Cheese Cream Frosting

- Cream cheese 125 grams
- Cocoa powder 1-2 tbsp.
- Granulated sweetener of choice 1-2 tbsp.

Directions

1. For the fudge brownies
2. Heat the oven up to 350 degrees, oil a loaf pan or small cake pan and put aside.

3. Melt the nut butter in a small microwave-proof bowl. In a big mixing bowl, put in the pumpkin puree, dark cocoa powder, nut butter, and combine very well.
4. Transfer the mixture to the oiled pan and put in preheated oven for around 20 to 25 minutes or until fully baked. Remove from the oven, set aside to cool completely. When cooled, apply the frosting and chill for about 30 minutes to settle.

Preparing the cream cheese or protein frosting:

1. In a big mixing bowl, mix together all the ingredients and beat well. With a tablespoon. keep adding dairy-free milk till a frosting consistency is reached.
2. For the coconut chocolate ganache
3. In a microwave-proof bowl, combine all the ingredients and heat gradually until just mixed- whisk till a glossy and thick frosting remains.

8. Healthy Keto Chocolate Raspberry Mug Cake

Prep. Time: 1 minute

Cook Time: 1 minute

Servings: 1 serving

The serving size is 1 mug cake

Nutrition as per serving:

152kcal / 8g fat / 13g carbs / 8g fiber / 7g protein = 5g net carbs

Ingredients

- Coconut flour 1 tbsp.
- Granulated sweetener of choice 1 tbsp.
- Cocoa powder 2 tbsp.
- Baking powder 1/4 tsp
- Sunflower seed butter (or any seed or nut butter) 1 tbsp.
- Pumpkin puree 3 tbsp.
- Frozen or fresh raspberries 1/4 cup
- Coconut milk unsweetened 1-2 tbsp.

Directions

1. In a microwave-proof mug, put in the dry ingredients and stir well.
2. Add in the rest of the ingredients, except for milk and raspberries, and combine until a thick batter is formed.
3. Stir in the raspberries and add one tbsp. of milk. Add extra milk if the batter gets too thick. Place in microwave and cook for 1 to 2 minutes. Should come out gooey in the center. If you overcook, it will become dry.

Oven Directions

1. Heat oven up to 180C.
2. Oil an oven-proof ramekin. Add the prepared batter and put in the oven for 10-12 minutes, or until done.

9. Keto Avocado Brownies

Prep. Time: 10 minutes

Cook Time: 30 minutes

Servings: 12 squares

Nutrition as per serving:

155kcal / 14g fat / 13g carbs / 10g fiber / 4g protein = 2.8g net carbs

Ingredients

- Avocado, mashed 1 cup
- Vanilla 1/2 tsp
- Cocoa powder 4 tbsp.
- Refined coconut oil (or ghee, butter, lard, shortening) 3 tbsp.
- Eggs 2
- Lily's chocolate chips melted 1/2 cup (100 g)

Dry Ingredients

- Blanched almond flour 3/4 cup
- Baking soda 1/4 tsp
- Baking powder 1 tsp
- Salt 1/4 tsp
- Erythritol 1/4 cup (see sweetener note *1)
- Stevia powder 1 tsp (see sweetener note *1)

Directions

1. Heat the oven up to 350F/ 180C.
2. Sift together the dry ingredients in a small bowl and stir.
3. Place the Peeled avocados in a food processor and process until smooth.
4. One by one, add all the wet ingredients into the food processor, processing every few seconds
5. Now include the dry ingredients into the food processor and blend until combined.
6. Line a parchment paper in a baking dish (of 12"x8") and transfer the batter into it. Spread evenly and put in the heated oven. Cook for 30 minutes or the center springs back to touch. It should be soft to touch.

7. Remove from oven, set aside to cool fully before cutting into 12 slices.

10. Low Carb-1 minute Cinnamon Roll Mug Cake

Prep. Time: 1 minute

Cook Time: 1 minute

Servings: 1 serving

The serving size is 1mug

Nutrition as per serving:

132kcal / 4g fat / 6g carbs / 2g fiber / 25g protein = 4g net carbs

Ingredients

- Protein powder, vanilla flavor 1 scoop
- Baking powder 1/2 tsp
- Coconut flour 1 tbsp.
- Cinnamon 1/2 tsp
- Granulated sweetener 1 tbsp.
- Egg 1 large
- Almond milk, unsweetened 1/4 cup
- Vanilla extract 1/4 tsp
- Granulated sweetener 1 tsp
- Cinnamon 1/2 tsp

For the glaze

- Coconut butter melted 1 tbsp.
- Almond milk 1/2 tsp
- Cinnamon a pinch

Directions

1. Oil a microwave-proof mug. In a small bowl, add the protein powder, coconut flour, baking powder, sweetener, cinnamon and mix well.
2. Add in the egg and stir into the flour mixture. Include the vanilla extract and milk. If the batter is too dry, keep adding milk until a thick consistency is reached.
3. Pour this batter into the oiled mug. Sprinkle extra cinnamon and keto granulated sweetener over the top and swirl. Place in microwave and cook for 60 seconds, or till the center is just cooked. Do not overcook, or it will come out dry. Drizzle the glaze on top and enjoy!
4. Prepare glaze by mixing all ingredients and use.

11. Double Chocolate Muffins

Prep. Time: 10 minutes

Cook Time: 15 minutes

Servings: 12 muffins

The serving size is 1 muffin

Nutrition as per serving:

280 kcal / 27g fat / 7g carbs / 4g fiber / 7g protein = 3g net carbs

Ingredients

- Almond flour 2 cup
- Cocoa powder unsweetened 3/4 cup
- Swerve sweetener 1/4 cup
- Baking powder 1 1/2 tsp.
- Kosher salt 1 tsp.
- Butter melted 1 cup (2 sticks)
- Eggs 3 large
- Pure vanilla extract 1 tsp.
- Dark chocolate chips, sugar-free (like lily's) 1 cup

Directions

1. Heat oven up to 350° and line cupcake liners in a muffin tin. In a big bowl, stir together almond flour, Swerve, cocoa powder, salt and baking powder. Include eggs, melted butter and vanilla and mix until combined.
2. Stir in the chocolate chips.
3. Pour batter equally in muffin cups and bake for 12 minutes or until the muffin top springs back to touch.

Chapter 4- Keto Fat Bombs

1. Cheesecake Fat Bombs

Prep. Time: 5 minutes

Servings: 24Fat Bombs

The serving size is 1 Fat Bomb

Nutrition as per serving:

108kcal / 12g fat / 1g carbs / 1g fiber / 1g protein = 0g net carbs

Ingredients

- Heavy Cream 4 oz.
- Cream cheese at room temperature 8 oz.
- Erythritol 2-3 tbsp.
- Coconut oil or butter 4 oz.
- Vanilla extracts 2tsp.
- Baking chocolate or coconut for decorating

Directions

1. In a big mixing bowl, add all the ingredients and mix for 1-2 minutes with an electric mixer until well combined and creamy.
2. Spoon mixture into an unlined or lined mini cupcake tin. Chill for 1-2 hours in the refrigerator or freezer for about 30 minutes.
3. Take out from the cupcake tins and store them in a sealed container. It can be refrigerated for up to two weeks.

2. Brownie Fat Bombs

Prep. Time: 15 minutes

Servings: 16 fat bombs

The serving size is 2 fat bombs

Nutrition as per serving:

174 kcal / 16g fat / 4g carbs / 2g fiber / 3g protein = 2g net carbs

Ingredients

- Ghee 1/4 cup
- Cocoa butter 1 oz.
- Vanilla extract 1/2 tsp
- Salt 1/4 tsp
- Raw cacao powder 6 tbsp.
- Swerve Sweetener powdered 1/3 cup
- Water 2 tbsp.
- Almond butter 1/3 cup
- Nuts, chopped (optional) 1/4 cup

Directions

1. melt the cocoa butter and ghee together In a heat-safe bowl placed over a pot of simmering water,
2. Add in the sweetener, cacao powder, salt and vanilla extract. This mixture will be smooth and thin.
3. Stir in the water and beat the mixture till it thickens to the consistency of a thick frosting.
4. Mix in the nut butter with a rubber spatula. The mixture will look like cookie dough. Mix in the coarsely chopped nuts.
5. Shape into 1 inch sized balls (will make about 16) and chill until firm.

3. Coffee Fat Bombs

Prep. Time: 10 minutes

Servings: 8 Fat Bombs

The serving size is 1 Fat Bomb

Nutrition as per serving:

140 kcal / 14g fat / 4g carbs / 2g fiber / 1.5g protein = 2g net carbs

Ingredients

- Cream Cheese, Full-fat 8 Oz.
- Butter Unsalted, ½ cup (1 Stick)
- Instant Coffee 1 to 2 Tbsps.
- Chocolate Chips, Low Carb, heaped ¼ Cup
- Confectioners Erythritol heaped ⅓ Cup
- Cocoa Powder, Unsweetened 1½ Tbsp.

Directions

1. In a large bowl, place the butter and cream cheese (both should be at room temperature)
2. Combine them with an electric mixer until smooth.
3. Then include all the remaining ingredients in the bowl, blending until well-combined
4. Scoop out the batter with a tablespoon or a cookie scoop to make around 12 bombs. Place them on a baking sheet lined with parchment. Chill for about 3 hours.

4. Peanut Butter Fat Bombs

Prep. Time: 10 minutes

Servings: 12 fat bombs

The serving size is 1/2 fat bomb

Nutrition as per serving:

247 kcal / 24.3g fat / 3.2g carbs / 1.2g fiber / 3.6g protein = 2g net carbs

Ingredients

For fat bomb

- Natural peanut butter (no sugar) 3/4 cup
- Coconut oil (melted) 1/2 cup
- Vanilla extract 1 tsp.
- Liquid stevia 3 – 4 drops
- Sea salt 1/4 tsp.

For Ganache

- Coconut oil 6 tbsp.
- Cocoa powder 1 tbsp.
- Liquid stevia 1 – 2 drops

Directions

1. Mix the peanut butter, coconut oil, vanilla extract, salt, and liquid stevia together in a small mixing bowl, beat until creamy and smooth.
2. Line muffin paper cups in a six-cup-muffin tray. Fill each cup with about 3 tbsp. of the peanut butter mixture.
3. Refrigerate for about 1 hour to solidify.
4. Meanwhile, beat together the ingredients for Ganache until it's silky.
5. Drizzle about one tbsp. of the chocolate ganache on every fat bomb.
6. Chill for about 30 minutes and enjoy.

5. Cream Cheese Pumpkin Spiced Fat Bombs

Prep. Time: 10 minutes

Servings: 12 Fat Bombs

The serving size is 1 Fat Bomb

Nutrition as per serving:

80 kcal / 7.5g fat / 2g carbs / 0.25g fiber / 1.5g protein = 1.75g net carbs

Ingredients

- Pure pumpkin ⅔ cup
- Pumpkin pie spice ½ tsp
- Cream cheese, full-fat 8 oz.
- Butter melted 3 tbsps.
- Confectioner's erythritol 3 tbsps.

Directions

1. Place all the ingredients in a large bowl and mix with an electric mixer until combined.
2. Make 12 equal-sized balls from the dough. Place paper liners in a mini-muffin tin and place the PB cookie dough in the muffin tin.
3. Chill for a minimum of 2 hours

Note:

If the pumpkin pie spice is not available, make some with the following ingredients

¼ tsp cinnamon, a pinch of (each) - nutmeg, cloves, ginger and allspice.

6. Brownie Truffles

Prep. Time: 5 minutes

Cook Time: 5 minutes

Servings: 20 Truffles

The serving size is 1 Truffle

Nutrition as per serving:

97kcal / 8g fat / 5g carbs / 3g fiber / 4g protein = 2g net carbs

Ingredients

- Sticky sweetener, keto-friendly 1/2 cup of choice
- Homemade Nutella 2 cups
- Coconut flour 3/4 cup (or almond flour 1 ½ cup)
- Chocolate chips, sugar-free 2 cups

Directions

1. Combine the coconut/almond flour, sticky sweetener and chocolate spread in a big mixing bowl. Add a bit more syrup or liquid; if the mixture is too thick, it should become a creamy dough.
2. Place parchment paper on a large plate. Shape into small balls with your hands, and set on the plate. Chill.
3. Melt the sugar-free chocolate chips. Take the truffles from the refrigerator. Immediately, coat each truffle with the melted chocolate, making sure all are evenly coated.
4. Set back on the lined
5. Plate and chill until firm.

7. Coconut Strawberry Fat Bombs

Prep. Time: 10 minutes

Servings: 20 fat bombs

The serving size is 1fat Bomb

Nutrition as per serving:

132kcals / 14.3g fat / 0.9g carbs / 0g fiber / 0.4g protein = 0.9g net carbs

Ingredients

For Coconut base:

- Coconut cream 1 1/2 cups
- Coconut oil (melted) 1/2 cup
- Stevia liquid 1/2 tsp.

- Lime juice 1 tbsp.

For Strawberry topping:

- Fresh chopped strawberries 2 oz.
- Coconut oil (melted) 1/2 cup
- Liquid stevia 5 – 8 drops

Directions

Prepare the coconut base:

1. In a high-speed blender, place all the coconut base ingredients and blend them completely until combined and smooth.
2. Distribute the mixture evenly into an ice cube tray, muffin tray, or a candy mold, leaving room for the topping.
3. Chill in the freezer to set for about 20 minutes.

For the Strawberry topping:

1. In a blender, put all the ingredients for the strawberry topping, then blend until smooth.
2. When the base is set, spoon the strawberry mixture equally over each one.
3. Refrigerate the fat bombs for about 2 hours and enjoy.

8. Raspberry & White Chocolate Fat Bombs

Prep. Time: 5 minutes

Servings: 10-12 fat bombs

The serving size is 1 fat Bomb

Nutrition as per serving:

153kcal / 16g fat / 1.5g carbs / 0.4g fiber / 0.2g protein = 1.2g net carbs

Ingredients

- Cacao butter 2 oz.
- Coconut oil 1/2 cup
- Raspberries freeze-dried 1/2 cup
- Erythritol sweetener, powdered (like swerve) 1/4 cup

Directions

1. Place paper liners in a 12-cup muffin pan.
2. In a small pot, heat the cacao butter and coconut oil on low flame until melted completely. Take off the pot from heat.

3. Blend the freeze-dried raspberries in a blender or food processor, or coffee grinder.
4. Include the sweetener and powdered berries into the pot, stirring to dissolve the sweetener.
5. Distribute the mixture evenly between the muffin cups. Don't worry if the raspberry powder sinks to the bottom. Just stir the mixture when pouring them into each mold to distribute the raspberry powder in each mold.
6. Chill until hard. Enjoy.

9. Almond Joy Fat Bombs (3 Ingredients)

Prep. Time: 2 minutes

Cook Time: 3 minutes

Servings: 24 cups

The serving size is 1 cup

Nutrition as per serving:

72kcal / 8g fat / 6g carbs / 4g fiber / 2g protein = 2g net carbs

Ingredients

- Coconut butter softened 1/4 cup
- Chocolate chips, sugar-free, divided 20 oz.
- Almonds 24 whole

Directions

1. Place muffin liners in a 24-cup mini muffin tin and put them aside.
2. Melt 3/4 of the sugar-free chocolate chips in a microwave-proof bowl. Distribute the chocolate mixture equally into all the muffin liners. Also, scrape down all the chocolate coated on the sides. Chill until firm.
3. When the chocolate is hard, spoon in the melted coconut butter evenly into every chocolate cup, leaving room for chocolate filling on top. Add in more softened coconut butter if needed.
4. Melt the rest of the chocolate chips and with it, cover each of the chocolate coconut cups. Place an almond on top of each cup and chill until firm.

10. Pecan pie fat bombs

Prep. Time: 15 minutes

Servings: 18 balls

The serving size is 2 balls

Nutrition as per serving

121 kcal / 12g fat / 3.8g carbs / 2.9g fiber / 2g protein = 0.9g net carbs

Ingredients

- Pecans, (or any nut) 1½ cup s
- Coconut butter, ¼ cup
- Coconut shredded ½ cup
- Chia seeds 2 tbsp.
- Pecan butter (or any nut butter) 2 tbsp.
- Flax meal 2 tbsp.
- Coconut oil 1tsp.
- Hemp seeds 2 tbsp.
- Vanilla extract ½tsp.
- Cinnamon 1½tsp.
- Kosher salt ¼tsp.

Directions

1. Add the ingredients altogether in a food processor. Process for a minute or two to break down the mixture. First, it will become powdery. Then it will stick together but remain crumbly.
2. Continue to process until the oils begin to expel a bit, and the mixture will begin to stick together easily –be cautious not to process excessively, or you will have nut butter.
3. Using a tablespoon or small cookie scooper, scoop to make equal pieces of the mixture. Roll them into balls with your hands placing them all on a large plate. Chill for about 30 mins.
4. Keep in a sealed container or a zip-lock bag in the freezer or refrigerator.

11. PB. Cookie Dough Fat Bomb

Prep. Time: 10 minutes

Servings: 12 Fat Bombs

The serving size is 1 Fat Bomb

Nutrition as per serving:

135kcal / 11g fat / 5g carbs / 3.5g fiber / 4g protein = 1.5g net carbs

Ingredients

- Lily's chocolate chips ⅓ cup

- Almond flour, superfine 1 cup
- Natural peanut butter 6 tbsps.
- Confectioner's erythritol 2 tbsps.
- Coconut oil (melted) 1 tbsps.
- Vanilla extract 1 tsp
- Salt, a pinch

Directions

1. Place all the ingredients in a large bowl and mix with a spoon until crumbly.
2. Form a dough ball with your hands.
3. Line parchment paper on a baking sheet. Scoop out equal-sized 12 cookie dough fat bombs.
4. Chill for about an hour
5. Once they are done setting, keep in a sealed bag in the fridge

Conclusion

When going on a ketogenic diet, one retains modest protein consumption but increases their fat intake. The transition to a low-carb diet brings your body into a ketosis state, where fat is used for energy compared to carbohydrates.

It takes some time for fats to decompose through the digestive tract and delay the decomposition of the carbohydrates into sugar, maintain our blood sugar concentrations steady and allow us to feel satiated longer. Based on observational evidence, incorporating a tablespoonful of coconut oil into your diet every day may also result in lower weight.

You may also need to monitor the portion sizes, but as fat is intrinsically pleasing, having one for breakfast will help deter eating during meals.

When consuming high-fat meals, including keto fat bombs, you will further encourage weight reduction by decreasing appetite for the next meal. Be it fat bombs or cheesy waffles or any other hi fat low-carb dessert, they are a dieter's dream come true.

Following the keto diet can positively impact one's brain function.

Advantages of the ketogenic diet and fat bombs.

Keto fat bombs may be seen as a way to reduce sugar habits.

Ketogenic fat bombs are simple to produce, easy to keep, and easy to eat; they often need fewer ingredients than other foods.

Ketogenic fat bombs are tasty and have a broad variety of low-carb recipes.

Ketogenic fat bombs are quick to produce, are easy to store, and are ready to consume at any time.

In this book, you will find the best and easy to prepare keto cakes, chaffles, and yummy high-fat recipes that will fulfill your cravings for desserts after meals or snacks when you don't feel too hungry. Enjoy these recipes by yourself, or even better, share the joy with family and friends!

Keto Bread Machine Cookbook 2021 with Pictures

Choose between 25+ Keto Hands-Off Recipes and Bake Homemade Bread that Make Everyone Envy

By

Jamie Carter

Table of Contents

Introduction

Bread is the most prominent food in almost every household around the globe. Bread is commonly a product of baking consists of numerous kinds of doughs, buns, and crusts. Usually, all kinds of bread dough are made from flour, yeast, and water in different shapes, methods, and flavors. The main process evolves around mixing and blending until they turned into a rigid paste or dough and then baked into a bread, loaf, or bun form afterward.

If we go through history, we will see that bread is one of the oldest food made and consumed by human beings since the beginning of agriculture. It plays a noteworthy role in religious rituals and cultural life, and language. Bread has a lot of significant roles as a meal around the world. It is consumed differently in different cultures, most often as a side meal, snacks, breakfast, lunch, or dinner or even combined as an important ingredient in different food/cuisine preparations.

Freshly homemade bread is one of the most satisfying things to eat and make. Although because of hectic life routines and busy schedules, most people have never even tried making homemade bread in their lives. But a lot has begun to change with the arrival of automatic bread machines you can easily make bread at the convenience of your home without spending a lot of time.

One of the best things about making your homemade bread is that you can always opt for healthy ingredients; unlike bread, you buy from outside when you make homemade fresh bread. You can always customize your list of ingredients, be it nuts of your choice, almond or coconut flour, gluten-free bread, nutritional yeast, or any other sort of restrictive ingredients.

Now the main question arises what a bread machine is? How does the bread machine work? How many kinds of bread can you make with a bread machine? Or is the bread machine worth buying?

An automatic home appliance for turning uncooked ingredients into dough or baked bread is called a bread machine. A bread machine is made up of a baking pan, built-in paddles at the bottom of the pan seated in a small oven center. The bread machine usually comes up with a small built-in screen called a control panel. You can adjust your choice of preferences while baking bread using settings input via the control panel.

Usually, the different bread machine comes up with different instructions. It may take some time to read the full instructions of your machine. But you will get a whole idea about the operating, cleaning, and safety features of the machine. Besides operating and other options manual will also provide a selection of recipes that are tested. If you are new to breadmaking, these recipes particularly are an excellent way to start.

The traditional order of ingredients starts with liquids and finishes with the dry ingredients, the fat, and then the yeast, though there may be some exceptions. The yeast is held away from the fluids not to activate until it starts to knead.

There are many different programs for producing many different styles of the loaf for most bread makers. Using various types of flour and varying the other ingredients, you can produce white bread, pizza whole meal, or special loaves. On its display screen, you can see the numerous choices this beadmaker offers (from the top: basic, whole meal, multigrain, French, pizza, cake, dough, and bake only). You put a slightly different mix into the tin at the beginning for different breads and choose a different program from the show. The bread machine can automatically manage various kneading, growing and baking times, and so on. You can use the bread machine to make different kinds of dough by choosing the dough cycle option from the control panel then baking it in the oven in any shape or form you like. From bun to baguettes, to pizza pull-apart, if you prefer a particular shape or bread style.

Nowadays bread machine is a very helpful and essential tool for most busy people. It has transformed baking bread into a hand-off process. From kneading to baking, the bread machine does all the job. Just measure and put all the ingredients in the baking pan, close the lid, start the button, and you are done. It feels magical if you own a bread machine. Without any extra effort, you can enjoy fresh homemade bread any day or at any time of the week, and it is worth investing your money in.

Chapter 1: Bread Machine Breakfast Recipes

1.1 Simple Flaxseed Keto Bread

Total time of cooking

3 hours 10 minute

Servings

5

Nutrition facts

Calories 263 (for two slices)

Fat 18g

Protein 12g

Net carbs 4g

fiber 10g

total carbs 14g

Ingredients:

This is the list of ingredients required to make simple flaxseeds keto bread.

- 1 cup of almond flour
- 1/4 cup of brown flaxseeds
- 1/3 cup of coconut flour
- 1 teaspoon of active dry yeast
- 2 tablespoons of psyllium husk powder
- 1/2 teaspoon of baking soda

- 1/2 teaspoon of salt

- 3 egg whites

- 1 whole egg

- 1 cup of warm water

- 1 teaspoon of olive oil

Instructions:
Follow the instructions mentioned below to make flaxseeds keto bread.

1. Sift the flour first to remove lumps.

2. First, add warm water to the bread machine pan, and sprinkle active dry yeast on top .

3. Wait for the yeast to activate.

4. Approximately After 5 minutes, add all the other ingredients into the bread machine pan.

5. Press the basic cycle option from your bread machine and choose medium crust.

6. When baking is finished, wait for few minutes before you remove bread from the pan.

7. slice and enjoy

1.2 Keto Coconut white bread (grain, gluten, and sugarfree)

Total time of cooking
3 hours 50 minutes

Servings
20 servings
Nutrition facts
Calories 56 (per serving)

Fat 4g

Protein 2.4g

Net carbs 1.2g

Ingredients:
Here is the list of ingredients required to make keto coconut white bread.

- 1 1/2 (180g) cups of almond flour

- 7 large eggs at room temperature

- 3 tablespoon (43 g) of apple cider vinegar

- 3.75 tablespoon (33g) of finely grounded psyllium husk powder

- 4 teaspoon (12g) of instant yeast

- 1 1/2 (360g) of lukewarm water

- 4 teaspoon (18g) of baking powder

- 1 teaspoon of salt

- 3 tablespoon (45g) of olive or coconut oil optional

Instructions:

Follow the instructions mentioned below to make keto coconut white bread.

1. Assemble all the ingredients.

2. Place the kneading paddles in the bread machine pan.

3. Follow your bread machine recommended order and add all of the above ingredients. Sprinkle yeast on top of the ingredients to ensure that it does not come into contact with other liquid ingredients.

4. Choose gluten-free and medium crust in the settings press the start button.

5. When the baking time is over, click the stop button.

6. Remove the baking pan from the bread machine to cool down for a while before removing the bread.

7. After a while, when it is cooled down, give your baking pan a toss and slightly remove bread from the pan.

8. bread is ready to serve.

1.3 Light and fluffy keto flaxseed buns

Total time of cooking

55 minutes

Servings

4 servings

Nutrition facts

Calories 232 (per serving)

Fat 11.9g

Protein 10.6g

Fiber 13.6g

Net carbs 2.1

Total carbs 15.7g

Ingredients:

Here is the list of ingredients required to make light and fluffy keto flaxseed buns.

- 1 1/4 (150g) cups of golden grounded flaxseeds
- 4 large egg whites or 2 whole egg at room temperature
- 2 tablespoon (28 g) of apple cider vinegar
- 1 teaspoon of psyllium powder
- 1/4 to 1 teaspoon of salt
- 2 teaspoon (8g) of baking powder
- 50 ml/0.2 cup of hot boiling water

Instructions:

Follow the instructions mentioned below to make light and fluffy keto flaxseed buns

1. Assemble all the ingredients.
2. As recommended by your bread machine, add all of the above ingredients. Add water, apple cider vinegar, golden flaxseeds grounded, psyllium powder, eggs, baking powder, and salt.
3. Choose the dough cycle option from the settings and press the start button.
4. When the dough cycle is over, click the stop button.
5. Remove the dough from the bread pan and divide the dough into 90 g portions each evenly. You will have more buns if you will make smaller portions.
6. Turn on the oven. At 350 F or 180 C, preheat your oven.
7. As the dough is sticky, so make sure to wet your hands before shaping it into balls. Now make balls and place them over a baking tray lined with parchment paper.
8. Sprinkle the top of the bun with seeds or herbs of your choice.
9. Place the baking tray in the oven. And bake for around 30 minutes or until golden brown. Touch and see if buns feel light and hollow upon touching it's done.
10. Remove from oven and serve.

1.4 Keto banana almond bread

Total time of cooking

4 hours

Servings
12 servings

Nutrition facts
Calories 173 (per serving)

Fiber 2.5g

Protein 3.9g

Net carbs 2.3g

Fat 14.9g

Ingredients:

Here is the list of ingredients required to make keto banana almond bread.

- 3/4 (84g) cups of coconut flour
- 1/2 (120ml) cups of heavy whipping cream at room temperature
- 1/2 cup + 1 tablespoon (130g) melted unsalted butter at room temperature
- 5 large eggs at room temperature
- 1/2 (100g) cup of granulated sweetener
- 2 teaspoons (10 ml) of banana extract
- 1/4 teaspoon (1g) of salt
- 2 teaspoons (8g) of baking powder
- 1 teaspoon (3g) of ground cinnamon
- 1 teaspoon (5ml) of vanilla extract
- 1 cup of chopped almonds

Instructions:

Follow the instructions mentioned below to make keto banana almond bread.

1. Assemble all the ingredients.
2. As suggested by your bread machine, add all of the above ingredients in the bread machine baking pan except almonds.
3. Check dough after 5 minutes. If required, add 1 to 2 tbsp of water or flour according to the consistency of the dough.
4. When the machine beep, add almonds 5 to 10 minutes before the kneading cycle completes.

5. Choose the baking option according to the instructions of your bread machine.

6. Select the loaf size and crust color from the bread machine settings.

7. Once the baking is completed, transfer the bread into the oven rack and let it cool down for some time.

8. Cut into slices, top up with your favorite keto low carb syrup and enjoy.

1.5 Easy Keto Egg Loaf(How to make a keto French toast from an egg loaf)

Total time of cooking

55 minutes

Servings
4

Nutrition facts

Calories 232(per slice for egg loaf only)

Protein 5.7g

Net carbs 2.5g

Fat 20.6g

Ingredients:

Here is the list of ingredients required to make keto egg loaf.

- 4 tablespoons of melted butter

- 1/4 cup of coconut flour

- 4 whole eggs

- 8 oz cream cheese

- 3 tablespoons of any sweetener of your choice

- 1/4 cup of heavy whipping cream

- 2 teaspoons of baking powder

- 1 teaspoon of vanilla extract

- 1 teaspoon of cinnamon powder

Ingredients for keto French toast egg dip:
- 2 medium-sized eggs

- 1/2 tablespoon or 8 grams of unsweetened vanilla almond milk

- 1/2 tablespoon or 8 grams of keto maple syrup
- pinch of cinnamon powder

Instructions:
Follow the instructions mentioned below to make keto egg loaf

1. Put all the egg loaf ingredients in the bread machine pan, select the dough option from your bread machine menu and press the start button. After five minutes, check the dough if water or flour is needed.

2. Lined loaf pan with parchment paper, pour the egg loaf mixture into loaf pan and even out the top surface of egg loaf with a spatula's help.

3. Bake an egg loaf at 350 f for around 45 minutes or check with a toothpick.

4. Remove the loaf from the pan.

5. Before cutting it into slices, let the bread cool down on the baking rack for a while.

Instructions to make French toast egg dip

6. Take a small-size mixing bowl and break two medium eggs in it.

7. Add 1/2 tablespoon of unsweetened vanilla almond milk, 1/2 tablespoon of keto maple syrup, and a pinch of powdered cinnamon. Whisk with a fork until eggs are fully combined with other ingredients.

8. Dip the bread slices one by one into egg dip from both sides.

9. Turn on the stove and place the pan over medium heat, coat it with baking spray and cook bread from both sides until crispy or golden brown.

10. Serve your French toast with fruits and keto maple syrup.

1.6 Low Carb Keto Bagels

Total time of cooking
45 minutes

Servings
8

Nutrition facts
Calories 298(per bagel)

Protein 18g

Net carbs 5g

Fat 23g

Ingredients:
Here is the list of ingredients required to make keto bagels.

- 3 cups of shredded mozzarella cheese
- 2 oz cream cheese
- 3 large eggs (reserved one egg for egg wash)
- 1 1/3 cup of almond flour
- 1 tablespoon of baking powder
- for topping sesame seeds cheese or bagel seasoning (optional)

Instructions:

Follow the method mentioned below to make low-carb keto bagels.

1. Assemble all the ingredients.

2. In a safe microwave bowl, melt together mozzarella and cream cheese in 30 second intervals. Check after every 30 seconds, stir until cheese is completely melted. You can also melt cheese in a double boiler over the burner.

3. Now, place all the ingredients, including melted cheese, in the bread machine pan, select dough from settings, and press the start button.

4. Once the dough cycle is finished, take the dough out of the bread machine. The dough will be very adhering, which is ok.

5. Wrap pastry board with plastic wrap. Coat your hands with oil, and divide your dough into 8 equal sections. Now roll each dough section on the pastry board to make 1-inch thick dough ropes. The plastic wrap will prevent your dough from sticking to the board.

6. Make the circle shape with a 1-inch thick rope and pinch the ends shut.

7. Place bagels carefully on a baking sheet lined with parchment paper .place each bagel from a distance of 1 inch at least.

8. Now coat the top surface of bagels with an egg wash at this stage. If you want to add any bagel toppings, you can.

9. In a preheated oven, bake the bagels in the middle rack of the oven for around 14 to 15 minutes or until it turns golden brown.

10. Before removing it from the baking tray, allow the bagels to cool down.

1.7 Keto Raspberry and Lemon Loaf(grain, sugar, and gluten-free)

Total time of cooking
4 hours

Servings
12

Nutrition facts
Calories 166 (per slice)

Protein 5.7g

Fiber 2.5g

Net carbs 2.8g

Fat 14.7g

Ingredients:
Here is the list of ingredients required to make keto raspberry and lemon loaf.

- 4 tablespoons of sour cream

- 4 tablespoons of melted butter

- 2 whole eggs

- 200 grams of almond flour

- 1.5 teaspoon of baking powder

- 1 teaspoon of lemon essence/extract.

- 1 teaspoon of vanilla extract

- 1/4 cup of sugar substitute

- 100 grams of raspberries halved

Instructions:

Follow the method mentioned below to make keto raspberry and lemon loaf.

1.Assemble all the ingredients.

2.In the bread machine pan, add all the ingredients except raspberries and select the basic setting for bread and medium crust color, press start.

3.Prior to 5 minutes before the kneading cycle finishes, add raspberries(your machine will beep as a signal).

4.Bread machine will beep once the baking is done.

5.Remove bread pan from baking machine. Turn the bread pan upside down, give it a toss to remove bread easily place on baking rack let it cool down for few minutes before slicing.

6.serve.

1.8 Keto Peanut Butter Donut Recipe(grain, sugar, and gluten-free)

Total time of cooking
45 minutes

Servings
8

Nutrition facts
Calories 175 (per donut)

Protein 7g

Carbs 5g

Fiber 2g

Net carbs 3

Fat 14g

Ingredients:
Here is the list of ingredients required to make a keto peanut butter donut recipe.

- 1 and 1/4 cup of almond flour

- 1/2 cup of sugar substitute

- 1/3 cup and 2 tablespoons of unsweetened vanilla almond milk

- 5 tablespoons of no sugar added peanut butter

- 2 large eggs

- 1 teaspoon of baking powder

- 1/2 teaspoon of vanilla extract

- pinch of salt

For donut glaze
- 4 tablespoons of powdered peanut butter

- 3/4 tablespoon of confectioners' sugar

- 2 1/2 tablespoon of water

Instructions:
Follow the method mentioned below to make keto peanut butter donuts.

1.Assemble all the ingredients.

2.In the bread machine pan, add all the ingredients except unsweetened vanilla almond milk in the order mentioned by your bread machine—select the dough option from the control panel and press the start button.

3.Place dough in a large mixing bowl and add 1/3 cup of unsweetened vanilla almond milk. Fold it in the batter until it combines with dough and pourable batter forms.

4.Coat a donut pan with baking spray and pour the batter into the donut tray.

5.Place donut pan in the oven bake at 350 f for around 15 to 16 minutes.

6.Remove the donut pan out of the oven and let them cool down for few minutes.

Instructions for donut glaze:
1.For a donut glaze, add powdered peanut butter, confectioner sugar, and water in a bowl.

2.Mix well until a thick peanut butter glaze starts to form.

3.Add glaze layer on a donut.

4.Add toppings of your choice over donut glaze (you can use crushed peanuts or no-sugar-added chocolate chips.

1.9 Easy and Yummy Keto Blueberry Bread

Total time of cooking
5 hours

Servings
6

Nutrition facts
Calories 216 (per slice)

Protein 6g

Sugar 1g

Carbs 6g

Fiber 2g

Net carbs 4g

Fat 20g

Ingredients:
Here is the list of ingredients required to make a keto blueberry bread
- 1 cup of almond flour blanched

- 1/3 cup of blueberries

- 1/4 cup of coconut oil softened

- 2 large eggs at room temperature

- 1/2 cup of erythritol

- 2 tablespoons of canned coconut milk

- 1 teaspoon of vanilla extract

- 2 teaspoon bread machine yeast

Instructions:
Follow the method mentioned below to make keto blueberry bread.

1.Assemble all the ingredients.

2.In the bread machine pan, add all the ingredients except blueberries in the order mentioned by your bread machine.

3.Choose a basic cycle and medium crust from the settings.

4.Add blueberries when the bread machine beep, around five minutes before kneading completes.

5.Let it bake until the machine beeps.

6.When done, take out bread from the baking pan carefully and let it cool completely before serving.

7.slice and enjoy.

1.10 Low-Carb Keto Chocolate Breakfast Loaf

Total time of cooking
2 hours 40 minutes

Servings
12

Nutrition facts
Calories 133 (per slice)

Protein 4g

Carbs 5.5g

Fiber 3g

Net carbs 2.5g

Fat 10.5g

Ingredients:
Here is the list of ingredients required to make a low-carb keto chocolate breakfast loaf.

- 6 tablespoons of salted butter

- 4 eggs large

- 1/3 cup heaping full fat sour cream

- 1 1/3 cup almond flour

- 2/3 cup of sugar substitute

- 1/4 cup cocoa powder(unsweetened)
- 1 teaspoon vanilla extract
- 2 1/2 tablespoon keto chocolate chips
- 2 teaspoon instant yeast

Instructions:
Follow the method mentioned below to make low-carb keto chocolate breakfast loaf.

1.Add all the ingredients except chocolate chips to the bread machine pan. Follow the order recommended by your bread machine.

2.choose dough cycle from the settings panel. start press.

3.Add chocolate chips five minutes before the kneading cycle completes. (when the machine beeps as a signal).

4.When the dough cycle ends, remove the dough from the bread machine pan.

5.Coat loaf pan with baking spray and line with parchment paper.

6.Evenly spread the dough into the loaf pan and sprinkle keto chocolate chips at the surface of the loaf.

7.Bake it for around 50 minutes at 350 f in the preheated oven.

8.Insert a toothpick to check if your loaf is raw or done if it comes out clean, your loaf is done.

9.Cool it for a while before slicing.

1.11 Keto Rye Bread

Total time of cooking
2 hours 40 minutes

Servings
18

Nutrition facts
Calories 107 (per slice)

Protein 9.4g

Carbs 1.94g

Fiber 1.66g

Net carbs 7.44g

Fat 5g

Ingredients:
Here is the list of ingredients required to make keto rye bread.

- 1/2 cup of oat fiber

- 2 eggs beaten (at room temperature)

- 1.25 cups of vital wheat gluten

- 1 cup of warm, strong coffee

- 2/3 cup of flaxseed meal

- 2 tablespoons of unsweetened cocoa powder

- 2 tablespoons of erythritol powdered sweetener

- 2 tablespoons of butter(at room temperature)

- 1 tablespoon of caraway and 1 tablespoon of dill seeds

- 1 tablespoon active dry yeast

- 1 teaspoon honey

- 1 teaspoon pink Himalayan salt

- 1/2 teaspoon xanthan gum

Instructions:

Follow the method mentioned below to make keto rye bread.

1.Grab your container out of your bread machine.

2.Add all the ingredients (warm coffee, eggs, oat fiber, flaxseed meal, vital wheat gluten, add salt, erythritol, honey, xanthan gum, and butter around the outside edge of bread container not directly in the middle)now add active dry yeast, make a hole in the middle of dry ingredients, and add active dry yeast in the middle of the little hole to make sure the yeast does not come in contact with liquid ingredients. At the top of the mixture, add cocoa powder, caraway seeds, and dill seeds.

3.Put back the container in the bread machine, close the lid, and select basic white bread settings and dark crust from your machine control panel.

4.When the bread is done, remove it from the pan and cool it for a while on the oven rack.

5. slice and enjoy.

1.12 Soft And Fluffy Keto Walnut And Chocolate bread

Total time of cooking
2 hours 10 minutes

Servings
21

Nutrition facts
Calories 66 (per slice)

Protein 3g

Net carbs 1g

Fat 4.4g

Ingredients:

Here is the list of ingredients required to make walnut and chocolate bread.

- 3/4 cup of coconut flour

- 3/4 golden flaxseed grounded(use coffee bean grinder or multi grinder to make powder)

- 1/2 cup of erythritol

- 1/2 cup of dark chocolate (melted)

- 1/2 cup chopped walnuts(reserved half for topping and half for bread)

- 1 cup of hot water

- 3 tablespoons of psyllium husk powder(grounded in finer texture)

- 3 tablespoons of apple cider vinegar

- 9 large egg whites

- 3 teaspoons of baking powder

- 1 teaspoon of salt

Instructions:

Follow the method mentioned below to make keto walnut and chocolate bread.

1.Assemble all the ingredients.

2.Add all the ingredients except walnuts to the bread machine container in the order suggested by your bread machine.

3.Choose basic dough settings and press the start button. After kneading for few minutes, check the consistency of the dough and add one tablespoon of water or flour if required.

4.Five minutes prior to the last kneading, when the machine beeps, add walnuts.

5.Remove the dough from the pan when the kneading cycle ends.

6.Warmed up your oven at 350 f or 180 c.

7.Coat 8x4 pan lined at the bottom with parchment paper with baking spray. Spread the dough evenly.

8.Coat the top of the bread with chopped walnuts.

9.Bake for around 60 minutes in the preheated oven.

10.Place a wooden skewer in bread to check if it comes out clean it is done.

11.Cool it down on the oven rack before slicing.

12.Serve and enjoy.

1.13 Best Keto Coffee Cake

Total time of cooking
2 hours

Servings
16

Nutrition facts
Calories 167 (per slice)

Protein 3g

Net carbs 2g

Fat 16g

Total carbs 3g

Sugar 1g

Ingredients:
Here is the list of ingredients required to make keto coffee cake.

For the coffee cake batter:

- 1 1/2 cup of almond flour

- 1/2 cup of any keto sweetener

- 1/4 cup of heavy cream or coconut cream

- 1/3 cup of unsweetened almond milk

- 1/2 cup of melted butter or coconut oil

- 4 medium eggs at room temperature

- 2 tablespoons of coconut flour

- 2 teaspoons of baking powder
- 1/4 teaspoon of salt
- 2 teaspoons of vanilla extract

For the crumb topping:
- 1 cup of almond flour
- 1/2 cup of keto powdered sweetener
- 1/4 cup of soft butter or coconut oil
- 1/2 cup of nuts of your choice
- 1 teaspoon of ground cinnamon powder

For the cinnamon sugar:
- 1/4 cup of powdered sweetener
- 1 tablespoon of almond flour
- 1 teaspoon of ground cinnamon powder

For the sugar-free glaze:
- 1/3 cup of powdered erythritol
- 4 to 5 tablespoons of heavy cream
- 1 teaspoon of vanilla extract

Instructions:
Follow the method mentioned below to make keto coffee cake
1. Assemble all the ingredients.

2. Add all the ingredients of the coffee cake batter mentioned in the list into the bread machine container and select dough cycle.

3. During kneading, check the dough add water or flour if required according to the consistency of the dough.

4. When the machine beeps. Remove the dough from the bread machine.

5. At 350 f or 180 c preheat your oven.

6. For Crumb Topping:

Combine all of the crumb topping ingredients with the help of a fork until the mixture becomes crumbly.

7. For Cinnamon Sugar:

Take a bowl and mix together almond flour, ground cinnamon powder, and sweetener. Keep it aside.

8. Line a 9x9 inches square cake pan with parchment paper.

9. For assembling the first spread half of the cake batter to the pan. Now add a layer of cinnamon sugar and then again spread the remaining cake batter. Over the top of the cake, evenly spread

crumb mixture.

10.Place the baking pan in preheated oven and bake for around 35 to 40 minutes or until of cake is golden browned.

11.Now, prepare a sugar-free glaze. Mix all the ingredients to make a sugar-free glaze until the glaze thickens, and powdered erythritol is dissolved.

12.Cut the cake into 16 slices and drizzle the glaze over the top of the coffee cake.

13.Serve and enjoy.

1.14 Easy And Tasty Keto Yogurt Cake

Total time of cooking
2 hours 55 minutes

Servings
12

Nutrition facts
Calories 188(per serving)

Protein 7g

Carbs 6g

Fat 16g

Fiber 4g

Ingredients:
Here is the list of ingredients for yogurt bread.

- 2 cups of almond flour

- 1 cup of Greek yogurt

- 1/2 cup of granulated erythritol

- 1/3 cup of melted unsalted butter

- 3 large eggs

- 2 tablespoons of coconut flour

- 1 1/2 tablespoon of lemon juice

- 1 tablespoon of lemon zest

- 2 teaspoons of bread machine yeast

For glaze:
- 1/2 cup of powdered erythritol

- 2 to 3 tablespoons of water

- 1 tablespoon of lemon juice

Instructions:

Follow the method mentioned below to make keto yogurt bread.

1. Assemble all the ingredients.

2. In the bread maker pan, add all the ingredients of lemon bread and choose basic bread and medium crust from the control panel to start the machine.

3. Check the consistency of dough during kneading. If needed, add two tablespoons of water.

4. When the baking cycle ends, place bread on a cooling rack.

5. For the glaze, add powdered erythritol and lemon juice, and water into the bowl mix until all ingredients are well combined.

6. Slice the cooled bread and top up with glaze.

Chapter 2: Bread Machine Lunch Recipes

2.1 Keto Low Carb Naan Flatbread

Total time of cooking
40 minutes

Servings
3

Nutrition facts
Calories 530 (per flatbread naan)

Protein 28g

Carbs 6g

Fat 41g

Fiber 2g

Ingredients:
Here is the list of ingredients required to make keto low carb naan flatbread.

- 1 1/2 and another 1/4 cup of almond flour blanched

- 1 1/2 cups of shredded mozzarella full fat

- 2/3 cup of protein powder unflavored

- 1 egg beaten

- 1 1/2 tablespoons of full-fat sour cream

- 1 teaspoon of baking powder
- pinch of salt

Instructions:
Follow the method mentioned below to make keto low carb naan flatbread.

1.Assemble all the ingredients.

2.In a microwave-proof bowl, add mozzarella and sour cream and melt in 30 seconds of intervals until both ingredients are fully melted down.

3.Place all the ingredients in the bread machine container and select the dough cycle. After five minutes of kneading, check the dough consistency. If needed, add water or flour.

4.When the dough cycle finishes, remove the dough from the container and let the dough rest for 15 to 20 minutes.

5.Once the dough has rested, divide your dough into three portions equally and add water into your hands to prevent dough from sticking into your fingers.

6.Shape each ball into round flat naan bread.

7.On a baking sheet lined with parchment paper and place your naan bread dough and bake for 7 to 8 minutes and grill for 1 to 2 minutes from both sides in the oven until

golden brown color develops on the top of flatbread naan.

8.Serve fresh and enjoy.

2.2 Tasty And Delicious Keto Gingerbread Cake

Total time of cooking
3 hours

Servings
16

Nutrition facts
Calories 287 (per slice)

Protein 9.3g

Net carbs 4.3g

Fat 26.4g

Ingredients:
Here is the list of ingredients required to make keto gingerbread cake.

- 3 cups of almond flour
- 1/2 cup of keto brown sugar
- 2 to 3 tablespoons of ginger

- 1 tablespoon of ground cinnamon
- 3 teaspoons of baking powder
- 1 teaspoon of baking soda
- 1 teaspoon of ground cloves
- 1 teaspoon of salt
- 1 teaspoon of ground nutmeg
- 6 eggs
- 300 ml of whipping cream
- 60 g of melted butter
- 1 cup of chopped walnuts
- 1/4 cup sugar-free maple syrup (optional)

Instructions:

Follow the method mentioned below to make keto gingerbread cake.

1.Assemble all the ingredients.

2. Into bread machine container add all the wet ingredients and on top add dry ingredients except walnuts. Select a simple setting for dough. At nut signal, add walnuts five minutes before the last kneading period completes.

3.Select the cake option from settings, choose the medium crust, and press start.

4.When baking finishes, remove the cake from the pan and let it cool down for a while.

5.Slice and sprinkle powdered sweetener on the top of the cake.

2.3 Easy Keto Sourdough Bread Rolls Recipe

Total time of cooking
2 hours

Servings
8

Nutrition facts
Calories 263 (per bread roll)

Protein 12g

Net carbs 2g

Fat 20g

Fiber 10g

Carbs 12g

Ingredients:

Here is the list of ingredients required to make keto sourdough bread rolls.

- 1 1/2 cups of almond flour
- 1/2 cup of coconut flour
- 1/2 cup of flax meal
- 1/2 cup of apple cider vinegar
- 1/3 cup of psyllium husk
- 3/4 cup of egg whites
- 3/4 cup of buttermilk
- 1/2 cup of warm water
- 1 scoop of keto unflavored whey protein
- 2 whole eggs
- 3 tablespoons of melted butter
- 2 teaspoon of instant yeast
- 1 teaspoon of Italian seasoning
- 1 teaspoon of kosher salt

Instructions:

Follow the method mentioned below to make keto sourdough bread rolls.

1.In your bread machine container, add all the ingredients and select dough cycle from your bread machine control panel, and press start.

2.Check Dough during kneading. Add water or flour if required according to the consistency of the Dough.

3.when the kneading cycle finished. Remove Dough from bread machine container.

4.Preheat oven at 350 f.

5.Line a baking sheet with parchment paper.

6.Divide Dough into eight pieces and make small loaves/rolls using your hands.

7.With a sharp knife, mark cuts on the top of each roll. Bake for 35 minutes or until each bread roll turned golden brown.

8.Then remove the baking sheet from the oven and brush the top of each bread roll with melted butter, and sprinkle Italian seasoning on the bread roll as well.

9.Place back again in the oven for 2 to 3 minutes under the grill until rolls turned deep golden brown from the top in color. (keep checking them during grill, so they

don't burn)

10.Serve fresh and enjoy.

2.4 Keto Fathead Cinnamon Rolls

Total time of cooking

1 hour 45 minutes

Servings
5

Nutrition facts
Calories 290 (per cinnamon roll)

Protein 13g

Net carbs 5g

Fat 24g

Fiber 4g

Carbs 9g

Ingredients:
Here is the list of ingredients required to make keto fathead cinnamon rolls.

- 1 3/4 cups of almond flour(superfine)

- 3/4 cup of mozzarella cheese

- 3 tablespoons of coconut flour

- 3 tablespoons of confectioners erythritol

- 4oz cream cheese

- 1 large egg

- 2 teaspoons of instant yeast

Ingredients for cinnamon roll filling:

- 3 tablespoons of granulated erythritol

- 1 tablespoon of cinnamon powder

- 1 tablespoon of melted butter

Ingredients for icing:
- 1/4 cup of erythritol

- 1 tablespoon of vanilla almond milk

Instructions:
Follow the method mentioned below to make fathead cinnamon rolls.

1.Assemble all the ingredients.

2.Microwave cream cheese and mozzarella cheese in the microwave-proof bowl until melted.

3.Put all the ingredients of a cinnamon roll dough, including melted cheese mixture, into the bread machine container(first liquids, then dry ingredients on the top). Select dough cycle and press the start button.

4..Once the dough cycle ends, remove the dough from the container and place it on a floured surface and knead it with your hands for few minutes.

5.Use your hands to work with dough. Press out dough into an oval shape, do not use a rolling pin; otherwise, the dough will stick to the pin.

6.Make sure your dough is about 1/4 inch thick and 16 inches long. Now coat the top of the dough first with the melted butter and sprinkle granulated erythritol and cinnamon powder all over the dough. Now roll up the dough and cut it into five equal-sized pieces.

7.Leave rolls for 20 minutes to let them rise a bit.

8.Grease Parchment paper-lined baking sheet with baking spray.

9.At 350 f degrees, bake for around 20 minutes or until golden brown.

10.Remove rolls from the oven and let them cool down for few minutes.

11.Make icing for rolls. Take a bowl and add confectioners erythritol and almond milk and mix until dissolved.

12.Coat cinnamon rolls with icing and enjoy.

2.5 Mini Crispy Crust Keto Quiche With Filling

Total time of cooking
1 hour 15 minutes

Servings
6

Nutrition facts
Calories 470 (per slice)

Protein 14.5g

Net carbs 5.5g

Fat 44.2g

Fiber 4.2g

Carbs 9.7g

Ingredients:
Here is the list of ingredients required to make keto quiche crust.

- 1/4 cup of Coconut flour

- 1/4 cup of almond flour

- 1/3 cup of cold butter

- 1 large egg

- 1/2 teaspoon of salt

Ingredients for egg mixture:
- 3/4 cup of whipping cream

- 4 large eggs

- 1/2 teaspoon of black pepper

- 1/2 teaspoon of salt

Ingredients for filling:
- Mozzarella cheese

- Smoked salmon

- Dill for garnishing

Instructions:
Follow the method mentioned below to make keto quiche crust.

1.Assemble all the ingredients of the crust.

2.Add all the ingredients mentioned above for quiche crust in the bread machine pan.

3.Close the lid, choose dough cycle, and press the start button.

4.When the kneading period ends, remove the dough, make a ball out of the dough with your hands. wrap the dough with foil, flatten it and freeze it for around 15 minutes.

5.Take out the dough from the freezer after 15 minutes and divide it into six equal portions.

6.Grease mini pie pan with butter.

7.Shape pie dough using your hands.

8.To avoid air bubbles, prick holes with a fork.

9.Again, freeze for 15 minutes.

10.After 15 minutes, bake for 15 to 16 mins at 350 f or 180 c if the dough's center rises during baking. Press down with the back of the spoon.

For egg mixture:

11.In a bowl, add all ingredients of the egg mixture mentioned above and whisk until well mixed.

Assembling:

12.Place cheese and smoked salmon into the baked crust.

13.Pour the egg mixture on top, garnish with dill.

14.Bake for 20 minutes at 350 f or 180 c.

2.6 Keto Garlic Bread

Total time of cooking
3 hours

Servings
12

Nutrition facts
Calories 309 (per slice)

Protein 9g

Net carbs 5.5g

Fat 29g

Carbs 5g

Ingredients:
Here is the list of ingredients required to make keto garlic bread.

- 2 1/2 cups of Almond flour

- 1 1/2 cups of egg whites

- 2/3 cup of melted butter

- 1 1/2 tablespoon bread machine yeast

- 1 teaspoon of salt

Ingredients for topping:
- 1/2 cup of melted butter

- 1 tablespoon of dried parsley

- 2 teaspoons of garlic powder

Instructions:
Follow the method mentioned below to make keto garlic bread.

1.Assemble all the ingredients of the crust.

2.Add all the garlic bread items to the bread machine container—liquid ingredients on the bottom and dry ingredients on top. Just be careful to keep the yeast away from the liquid by putting yeast on top of dry ingredients.

3.Select basic bread cycle and medium crust from the settings panel and press the start button.

4.When baking is finished, remove bread from the pan and let it cool completely on the oven rack.

5.Cut down into 12 equal pieces.

6.For the topping, in a boiler, mix together butter, parsley, and garlic powder.

7.Spread topping on the bread evenly.

8.Again, place in the oven and broil for few minutes to crisp up the bread.

9.Serve.

2.7 Keto Coconut Crust Pizza (Eggless)

Total time of cooking
1 hour

Servings
10

Nutrition facts
Calories 74 (per slice)

Protein 2.6g

Net carbs 0.8g

Fat 5.8g

Ingredients:
Here is the list of ingredients required to make keto coconut crust pizza.

- 1/2 cup of coconut flour

- 1/2 cup of grounded golden flaxseeds or flaxseed meal

- 2 tablespoons of olive oil

- 2 tablespoons of finely grounded psyllium husk

- 1 tablespoon of Italian seasoning

- 2 teaspoons of active dry yeast

- 1/2 teaspoon of salt

- 240 ml hot or boiling water

Ingredients for pizza sauce:
- 200g canned peeled tomatoes

- 2 to 3 tablespoons of tomatoes paste
- 2 tablespoons olive oil
- 2 to 3 teaspoons salt
- 1 teaspoon dry basil
- 1 teaspoon onion powder
- 1 teaspoon dried parsley
- 1 teaspoon garlic powder
- 1 teaspoon black pepper
- 1 teaspoon oregano

(Blend all the ingredients, until smooth paste/sauce is formed)

Ingredients for topping:
- 180g vegan cheese
- 3 to 4 sliced button mushrooms
- 4 to 5 sliced black olives
- tricolor capsicum (cut into strips)
- chopped parsley for garnishing

Instructions:
Follow the method mentioned below to make keto coconut crust pizza.

1.Assemble all the ingredients of the crust.

2.In bread machine container, add yeast and hot water together and mix and let it sit for 10 minutes, so the yeast dissolves in water and becomes creamy in texture.

3.After 10 minutes, add olive oil, coconut flour, flaxseeds, psyllium husk, Italian seasoning, and salt.

4.Close the lid: select dough cycle, and press the start button.

5.Remove dough from the bread machine. Spread out in greased pizza pan.

6.Cover with cloth or towel and set aside for around 25 minutes for rising.

7.Prick holes with a fork to release air bubbles during bake for around 15 to 20 minutes on the lowest rack of your oven at 350 f or 180 c, then flip over the side and bake for another 5 minutes.

8.Remove pizza from the oven, spread the pizza sauce, then add vegan cheese and all other ingredients mentioned in the topping list.

9.Bake again for 10 minutes on the middle rack of the oven.

10.Remove the pizza from the oven. When it's done, sprinkle chopped parsley all over the pizza.

11.Make slices with a pizza cutter and serve.

2.8 Tasty And Easy Keto Cornbread

Total time of cooking
1 hour 10 minutes

Servings
12

Nutrition facts
Calories 254 (per serving)

Protein 8.4g

Carbs 6g

Fat 22.7g

Fiber 3g

Ingredients:
Here is the list of ingredients required to make keto cornbread.

- 2 cups of almond flour

- 1 cup of shredded cheddar cheese

- 1/2 cup of melted butter

- 1/4 cup of coconut flour

- 1/4 cup of sour cream

- 2/3 can of baby corn roughly chopped

- 3 large eggs

- 2 1/2 teaspoons of instant yeast

- 1 teaspoon of pink Himalayan salt

- 25 drops of liquid stevia

Instructions:
Follow the method mentioned below to make keto coconut crust pizza.

1.Assemble all the ingredients of the crust.

2.In the bread machine pan, add all the ingredients except baby corn, starting with liquid ingredients first and dry ingredients in the last).close the lid and select dough cycle. Add water or flour if required during kneading.

3.When the machine beeps, five minutes before final kneading begins, add chopped baby corn.

4.Remove dough from the pan. Spread in a casserole dish.

5.Bake for around 40 to 42 minutes in the preheated oven at 350 f.

6.Allow to cool down for few minutes before slicing.

7.Serve and enjoy.

2.9 Keto Tomato And Parmesan buns

Total time of cooking
1 hour 40 minutes

Servings
5

Nutrition facts
Calories 261 (per bun)

Protein 14.5g

Net carbs 4.9g

Fat 18.9g

Fiber 8.3g

Ingredients:
Here is the list of ingredients required to make keto tomato and parmesan buns.

- 1/2 cup of coconut flour

- 3/4 cup of almond flour

- 1/4 cup flax meal

- 1/3 cup chopped sun-dried tomatoes

- 2/3 cup of parmesan cheese

- 2 1/2 tablespoons of psyllium husk powder

- 2 tablespoons of sesame seeds

- 2 teaspoon of active dry yeast

- 1 teaspoon cream of tartar
- 1/2 teaspoon of salt
- 1 cup boiling water
- 3 large egg whites
- 1 whole egg

Instructions:
Follow the method mentioned below to make keto tomato and parmesan buns.

1.Add all the ingredients in the bread machine container except sun-dried tomato. Start with liquid ingredients first, and then add all the dry ingredients with yeast on top. Make sure yeast does not come in contact with liquid.

2.Select dough from the control panel and start the machine.

3.Remove dough from the bread machine and divide into five equal parts. Make balls with the help of your hands.

4.Place them with a 2 to 3 inches gap (buns will grow in size once baked) on a non-stick Baking sheet .let it rise for around 25 minutes. Sprinkle sesame seeds all over the bun.

5.At 350 f in the preheated oven, bake for 35 to 40 minutes.

6.Remove once done and cool on a baking rack before serving.

2.10 Eggless Keto Focaccia

Total time of cooking
1 hour 45 minutes

Servings
25

Nutrition facts
Calories 105 (per serving)

Protein 2.1g

Net carbs 1.6g

Fat 8.9g

Ingredients:
Here is the list of ingredients required to make an eggless keto focaccia recipe

- 2 1/2 cups of almond flour

- 1/3 cup of golden flaxseeds

- 1/2 cup of coconut flour

- 2 cups of hot boiling water

- 5 tablespoons of psyllium husk powder

- 2 teaspoons of bread machine yeast

- 1 teaspoon of salt

For oil mixture:
- 1/2 cup of olive oil extra virgin

- 3 to 4 cloves garlic (minced)

- 1 teaspoon of dried or fresh thyme

- 1 teaspoon of dried or fresh thyme

- 1/2 teaspoon of black pepper

- 1/2 teaspoon of salt

Instructions:
Follow the method mentioned below to make eggless keto focaccia.

1.Turn on your stove and cook all the items mentioned in the list for oil mixture in a small pot over low to medium heat and until garlic turns brown, then turn off the stove. Keep two tablespoons of oil mixture for greasing the baking pan, two tablespoons to brush the dough's top, and remaining to add in the dough.

2.In the bread machine pan, add all the ingredients of focaccia mentioned in the list of ingredients above, including the remaining oil mixture. And start the dough cycle when the dough cycle ends. Remove the dough from the pan.

3.With two tablespoons of oil mixture, brush the bottom of a deep-dish pizza pan. Spread the dough into a pan, flatten the dough using your hands. make as many dimples as you like with your fingers on the dough.

4.With two tablespoons of the reserved oil, brush the top of the dough.

5.Sprinkle some flaky salt and some fresh thyme and rosemary on top(optional).

6.At 350 f preheated oven bake for about 30 to 40 minutes on lowest rack.

7.Turn off the oven once ready and for around 30 minutes, let it sit in the oven to dry.

8.Once completely cool, cut into small squares and enjoy.

2.11 Keto Fathead Dough Stuffed Sausage Buns

Total time of cooking
1 hour

Servings
6

Nutrition facts
Calories 363(per serving)

Protein 19g

fiber 1g

Carbs 3g

Fat 30g

Ingredients:
Here is the list of ingredients required to make keto fathead dough stuffed sausage buns.

For fathead dough:
- 1 oz of cream cheese
- 3/4 cup of almond flour
- 1.5 cup of mozzarella cheese
- 12 oz ground breakfast sausage(pre-seasoned)
- 1 large egg
- 1 1/2 teaspoons of instant yeast

Instructions:
Follow the method mentioned below to make keto fathead dough stuffed sausage buns.

1.Assemble all the ingredients.

2.Melt cream cheese and mozzarella cheese in the microwave for 30 seconds.

3.In the bread machine pan, add all the ingredients except sausages, choose dough cycle, and press start.

4.When the dough cycle completes, take out the dough from the bread machine pan.

5.Warm up your oven at 400 F.

6.Turn on the stove and preheat a pan to medium-high heat.

7.Cut pre-seasoned sausage into six pieces equally, add to the hot pan and cook. Once cooked, set aside and let them cool down.

8.Divide your dough into six equal balls. Use your hands to flatten out each ball or either roll it. Place cooked sausage in the middle of the dough, wrap it, and make a ball with your hands. Repeat the procedure with all other dough balls.

9.On a baking sheet lined with parchment paper, place sausage balls, put seam side down.

10.Bake for around 15 to 20 minutes or until golden browned.

11.Serve.

2.12 Keto Chicken Pot Pie Turnover bread

Total time of cooking
1 hour 15 minutes

Servings
9
Nutrition facts
Calories 589(per serving)

Protein 37.9g

Net carbs 9.6g

Fat 45.7g

Ingredients:
Here is the list of ingredients required to make keto chicken pot pie turnover bread.

Ingredients for dough:
- 3 cups of almond flour
- 7 cups of mozzarella cheese
- 2 eggs
- 1 tablespoon of water
- 2 teaspoon of xanthan gum
- 2 teaspoon of instant yeast

Ingredients for pot pie mixture:
- 1/2 cup of diced onion
- 3 cups of shredded cooked chicken
- 1/2 cup red onion diced
- 1 cup chicken broth
- 3 tablespoons of freshly chopped parsley

- 1 tablespoon of coconut flour

- 8 oz mushrooms chopped

- 4 oz cream cheese

- 1 teaspoon thyme

- 3 minced garlic cloves

Instructions:

Follow the method mentioned below to make keto chicken pot pie turnover bread.

1.Assemble all the ingredients.

2.Add all the ingredients of dough mentioned in the list in the bread machine pan, close the lid, choose dough cycle, and start the machine.

3.Take the dough out of the bread machine when kneading finishes. Cover with a kitchen towel for around 20 to 25 minutes and let it rise.

4.Turn on the stove over medium-high heat melt butter in a large pan.

5.Add onion and cook for five minutes until it softens. Now add mushrooms, garlic, and thyme, sprinkle pepper and salt and cook for 5 minutes more until mushroom becomes tender.

6.Add coconut flour, whisk in the broth and proceed to cook for 3 to 5 minutes until the mixture thickens. Add chicken and turn the heat to low.

7.Add cream cheese and cook until cream cheese is fully melted. Add parsley and sprinkle salt. Remove from the stove and turn off the heat, and let it cool down.

8.To ensure all ingredients are fully combined, knead the dough with your hands.

9.Lay down parchment paper on a floured surface, place dough over it, put another parchment paper on top, and roll dough with a rolling pin into a rectangular shape (dough should be around 1/4 inches thick). Cut edges of the dough to form a perfect rectangular shape using a knife or pizza cutter. Cut further into nine tiny rectangles.

10.Place a spoonful of chicken pot pie mixture into each rectangle and fold over. Repeat the same procedure with other rectangles.

11.With egg brush, the tops of turnover bread.

12.Place turnovers in a non-stick baking sheet and bake for 20 minutes at 375 f degrees.

13.Serve and enjoy.

2.13 Keto Pecan Chocolate Pie

Total time of cooking
2 hour 15 minutes

Servings
8

Nutrition facts
Calories 504(per serving)

Protein 11g

Carbs 11g

Fat 49g

Fiber 7g

Ingredients:
Here is the list of ingredients required to make keto pecan chocolate pie.

For the sweet pie crust:
- 1.25 cups of almond flour

- 1/4 cup of cream cheese

- 3 tablespoons of unsalted butter

- 2 tablespoons of coconut flour

- 1 beaten egg

- 1/2 teaspoon of xanthan gum

- 1 teaspoon of instant yeast

- 1/4 pink Himalayan salt

- 15 drops of stevia

For the chocolate pie filling:
- 1 cup of heavy whipping cream

- 1 cup of raw chopped pecans

- 1/4 cup of butter

- 3 eggs large (room temperature)

- 4 oz unsweetened chocolate chopped

- 2 tablespoons of erythritol

- 1 teaspoon of vanilla extract

- 1/4 teaspoon of pink salt

- 1/4 teaspoon liquid stevia

Instructions:
Follow the method mentioned below to make keto chocolate pie.

1. Add all the sweet pie crust ingredients to the bread machine container. Select the dough cycle press the start button.

2.When kneading completes, remove dough from pan, make a ball of dough seal in plastic wrap, and freeze for at least 20 minutes.

3.Take out the dough after 20 minutes from the freezer. Place dough between two parchment papers, roll out the dough using a rolling pin, spread on the greased pie pan, flatten dough with your fingers, and prick holes using a fork in the crust.

4.Freeze again for 15 minutes.

5.At 350 F/180 C preheated oven, bake for 15 minutes or until it turns light brown.

6.Once done, allow the crust to cool down. Meanwhile, make the chocolate pie filling.

7.On a double boiler, heat butter, and heavy cream until it completely melts down, remove from the boiler and add the chocolate mix well until it turns smooth in texture. Add vanilla extract, erythritol, stevia, and salt and mix well until dissolved.

8.In a separate bowl, whisk eggs, add them into the chocolate mixture, and mix until completely blends.

9.Spread pecans on the bottom layer of cooled pie. Then pour the chocolate mixture on top and bake again for 20 minutes.

10.Before serving, let the tart cool for a while.

11. Before eating, sprinkle with unsweetened cocoa powder or powdered erythritol.

2.14 Starbucks Inspired Keto Poppy Seeds And Lemon Loaf

Total time of cooking
3 hour 40 minutes

Servings
12

Nutrition facts
Calories 201(per serving)

Protein 9g

Carbs 6g

Fat 17g

Fiber 3g

Ingredients:
Here is the list of ingredients required to make poppy seeds and lemon loaf.

- 2 1/8 cups of almond flour

- 1/2 cup of any sweetener

- 6 eggs large

- 3 tablespoons of unsalted melted butter

- 2 tablespoons of poppy seeds

- 2 tablespoons of lemon juice

- 1 1/2 heaping tablespoons of lemon zest

- 1 1/2 bread machine yeast

For Glaze:
- 1/2 cup of erythritol(powdered)

- 1 to 2 tablespoons of water

- 1 tablespoon of lemon juice

Instructions:
Follow the method mentioned below to make poppy seeds and lemon bread.

1.Combine all the ingredients in the bread machine container in the order suggested by your bread maker.

2.Pick basic bread and medium crust from the options of the bread machine control panel. And press the start button.

3.Check during kneading. Add two tablespoons of water if needed.

4.When baking finishes, remove bread from the bread machine container.

5.Leave it for 15 minutes to cool down before slicing.

6.For Glaze add lemon juice and erythritol to a bowl and slowly add water mix until fully incorporated.

7.Spread the Glaze over cooled bread slices and enjoy.

Chapter 3: Bread Machine Dinner Recipes

3.1 Keto Garlic Flatbread

Total time of cooking
1 hour 20 minutes

Servings
8

Nutrition facts
Calories 134(per serving)

Protein 7.7g

Net carbs 2.1g

Fat 9.9g

Ingredients:
Here is the list of ingredients required to make keto garlic flatbread.

Ingredients for dough:
- 1/2 cup of grated mozzarella cheese
- 1/2 cup of ground almonds or milled linseed
- 1 cup of courgette grated
- 1/3 cup of coconut flour

- 3 large eggs
- 1 1/2 teaspoons of bread machine yeast
- 1 teaspoon of garlic powder
- 1 teaspoon of mixed herbs
- 1 teaspoon of baking powder
- 1/4 teaspoon of xanthan gum
- 1/4 teaspoon of salt

For the garlic butter:
- 2 tablespoons of butter melted
- 1 to 2 garlic cloves (minced)

Instructions:
Follow the method mentioned below to make keto garlic flatbread.
1.Assemble all the ingredients.

2.Place keto garlic flatbread ingredients in the bread machine container, choose dough cycle, and start the machine. After five minutes of kneading, check the dough's consistency add one to two tablespoons of water if required.

3.Take out the dough from the bread machine once the dough cycle finishes. Grease your non-stick round pizza pan and spread the dough. Flatten the dough using your hands. leave it for 10 minutes to rise.

4.Place the baking pan in 350 degrees preheated oven and bake for around 25 to 30 minutes or until flatbread turns light golden brown.

5.Turn on your stove at low, medium heat. In a pan, heat butter first, then add minced garlic and cook until garlic turns nut brown.

6.Spread garlic butter mixture over the top of flatbread and brush evenly all over the baked flatbread.

7.Cut flatbread into eight slices and serve.

3.2 Simple And Tasty Keto Zucchini Bread

Total time of cooking
3 hours 20 minutes

Servings
14

Nutrition facts
Calories 186(per serving)

Protein 8.3g

Net carbs 2.7g

Fat 15.1g

Ingredients:

Here is the list of ingredients required to make keto zucchini bread.

- 1 1/2 cups of grated zucchini(courgette)
- 1/2 cup of ground almonds
- 3/4 cup of melted unsalted butter
- 2/3 cup of grated mozzarella cheese
- 2/3 cup of coconut flour
- 5 eggs large
- 2 teaspoons of bread machine yeast
- 1 teaspoon of dried oregano
- 1/2 teaspoon of xanthan gum
- 1/2 teaspoon of salt

Instructions:

Follow the method mentioned below to make keto zucchini bread.

1.Assemble all the ingredients.

2.Remove the Bread machine container. Add all the ingredients of zucchini keto bread to the container. Place the container into the bread machine, close the lid, select basic bread cycle and medium crust, and press the start button.

3.Check the dough consistency. After five minutes, add two tablespoons of water if required.

4.When the Baking period is finished. Remove the bread from the pan and place it into the cooling rack for some time.

5.Cut into slices and serve.

3.3 Low Carb Keto Pumpkin Spice Bread

Total time of cooking
3 hours

Servings
12

Nutrition facts
Calories 191(per serving)

Protein 7g

Net carbs 4g

Fat 16g

Total carbs 7g

Ingredients:
Here is the list of ingredients required to make pumpkin bread.

- 2 cups of almond flour

- 3/4 cup pumpkin puree

- 3/4 cup of erythritol

- 5 medium-sized eggs

- 4 tablespoons of softened butter

- 3 tablespoons of heavy whipping cream

- 2 tablespoons of coconut flour

- 3 teaspoons of pumpkin pie spice

- 1 1/2 teaspoons of instant yeast

- 1 teaspoon vanilla extract

Instructions:
Follow the method mentioned below to make keto pumpkin bread.

1.In a Bread machine container, add all the ingredients(liquids first followed by the dry ingredients in the end).

2.Select basic bread settings, medium crust, and loaf size. Start the machine.

3.After 5 minutes of mixing check dough, add 2 to 3 tablespoons of water required.

4.Once baking is done. Shift bread to a cooling rack and let it cool down completely.

5.Cut into 12 equal slices and serve.

3.4 Tasty And Easy Keto Olive Bread

Total time of cooking
2 hours

Servings
16

Nutrition facts
Calories 93(per serving)

Protein 3.5g

Net carbs 1.7g

Fat 6.4g

Ingredients:
Here is the list of ingredients required to make keto olive bread.

- 1 cup of hot water
- 3/4 cup of coconut flour
- 3 whole eggs
- 3/4 cup of golden flaxseed
- 3/4 cup of black olives(cut in small cubes)
- 3 tablespoons of psyllium husk (finely grounded)
- 3 tablespoons of apple cider vinegar
- 2 tablespoons of olive oil
- 2 teaspoons of instant yeast
- 1 teaspoon of salt
- 1 teaspoon of basil

- 1 teaspoon of ground oregano
- 1 teaspoon of thyme
- 1/2 teaspoon of garlic powder

Instructions:
Follow the method mentioned below to make keto olive bread.

1. Follow the order recommended by your bread maker, except olives add all the ingredients to the pan.

2. Choose your bread maker dough settings.

3. Five minutes before the last kneading cycle when the machine beeps, add olives

4. when the dough is formed, remove it from the bread machine.

5. Spread the dough evenly in the loaf pan lined with parchment paper.

6. Bake at 350 f at the middle rack of the preheated oven for 40 minutes .

7. Cooldown for sometime before slicing.

3.5 Classic Keto Meatloaf Recipe

Total time of cooking
2 hours 30 minutes

Servings
14

Nutrition facts
Calories 245(per serving)

Protein 13g

Net carbs 2g

Fat 19g

fiber 1g

Ingredients:
Here is the list of ingredients required to make keto meatloaf.

For meatloaf:
- 2 lbs ground beef

- 1 cup of almond flour

- 2 eggs large

- 1/2 chopped onion

- 4 garlic cloves (minced)

- 1 teaspoon of salt

- 1 teaspoon instant yeast

- 1/4 teaspoon of black pepper

For meatloaf sauce:
- 1/2 of cup tomato sauce (sugar-free)

- 2 tablespoons of mustard

- 2 tablespoons of vinegar

- 2 tablespoons of sweetener

- 2 tablespoons of olive oil

- 2 tablespoons of Worcestershire sauce

Instructions:
Follow the method mentioned below to make keto meatloaf.

1.Assemble all the ingredients.

2.In the bread machine container, add the eggs, almond flour, ground beef, garlic cloves, onion, black, salt, and instant yeast. Close the lid and select the dough option from the bread machine control panel.

2.During kneading, check the dough's consistency if required, add 2 to 3 tablespoons of water.

3.Turn off the bread machine once the dough cycle completes. Transfer the loaf mixture to a non-stick loaf pan.

4.Bake at 350 F/180 C for 35 minutes in the preheated oven.

5.Add all the ingredients in a medium mixing bowl mentioned in the list for meatloaf sauce. mix until combine .

6.Spread sauce evenly over top of the meatloaf. And bake for 40 minutes more.

7.Let it cool down for 15 minutes before serving.

3.6 Classic Keto Cheese Bread

Total time of cooking
4 hours

Servings
16

Nutrition facts
Calories 88(per serving)

Protein 3.25g

Carbs 2.25g

Fat 7.5g

fiber 0.3g

Ingredients:
Here is the list of ingredients required to make keto classic cheese bread.

- 1/4 cup of melted butter
- 1/2 cup of peanut flour
- 4 large egg yolks
- 5 oz cream cheese
- 2 tablespoons of golden monk fruit sweetener
- 1 teaspoon bread machine yeast
- 1 teaspoon Himalayan salt
- 1 teaspoon vanilla extract

Instructions:
Follow the method mentioned below to make keto classic cheese bread.

1.In order suggested by your bread maker. Add all the ingredients into the bread machine container (liquid ingredients first, then dry ingredients).

2.Choose basic bread settings and light crust also loaf size.

3.Start the machine check the dough during the kneading period. If needed, add two to three tablespoons of water.

4.Once baking is finished. Turn off the machine and let bread rest for few minutes.

5.Place bread on a cooling rack and leave it for 10 to 15 minutes.

6.Cut into 16 slices and enjoy.

3.7 Easy Keto Dinner Buns Low Carb

Total time of cooking
1 hour 50 minutes

Servings
8

Nutrition facts

Calories 170(per serving)

Protein 7g

Net Carbs 2g

Fat 13g

Ingredients:
Here is the list of ingredients required to make keto dinner buns.

- 1 1/4 cups of almond flour

- 1 cup of hot water

- 3 egg whites

- 5 tablespoons of psyllium husk powder

- 2 tablespoons of sesame seeds

- 2 teaspoons of bread machine yeast

- 2 teaspoons of vinegar

- 1/2 teaspoon of rock salt

Instructions:
Follow the method mentioned below to make keto dinner buns.

1.In order suggested by your bread maker. Add water, vinegar, egg whites, almond flour, psyllium husk powder, rock salt, and yeast(liquid ingredients first, then dry ingredients).

2.Choose dough cycle and start the machine.

3.Take out the dough from the pan once the dough cycle ends.

4.Divide dough into eight equal portions. And make balls with your hands. to prevent dough from sticking your hands, wet your hands a little before doing this.

5.Leave them for around 20 minutes to let them rise in size.

6.Place buns in a parchment paper-lined baking sheet with a 2 to 3 inches gap.

7.On top of each bun, sprinkle white and black sesame seeds.

8.Put in the oven preheated oven for 50 to 55 minutes at 350 F/ 180 C.

9.Let it cool down before eating.

3.8 Delicious And Easy Keto Tahini Almond Bread

Total time of cooking
2 hour 50 minutes

Servings
10

Nutrition facts
Calories 160(per serving)

Protein 7.3g

Carbs 0.6g

Fat 13.5g

Ingredients:
Here is the list of ingredients required to make tahini bread.

- 1 cup of tahini

- 1/2 cup of almond flour

- 2 large size eggs

- 1 1/2 tablespoons of lemon juice

- 2 teaspoons of chia seeds

- 1 teaspoon of vanilla extract

- 1 teaspoon of instant yeast

- 1 teaspoon of salt

Instructions:
Follow the method mentioned below to make tahini almond bread.

1. Add eggs, lemon juice, vanilla extract, tahini, almond flour, chia seeds, yeast, and salt into your bread machine container.

2.Close the bread machine's lid, pick the basic bread settings and medium crust, press the start button.

3.Once the bread is baked, let it rest few minutes in the bread machine.

4.Remove the bread from bread machine and transfer to oven rack for cooling purpose.

5.Once the bread is cooled down, slice and serve.

3.9 Keto Low Carb Savory Pie-Salmon Quiche

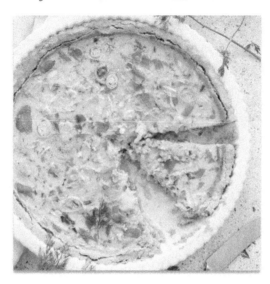

Total time of cooking
2 hour 20 minutes

Servings
10

Nutrition facts
Calories 320.42(per serving)

Protein 15.95g

Total Carbs 6.98g

Fat 25.54g

Fiber 3.02g

Sugar 1.4g

Ingredients:
Here is the list of ingredients required to make keto low-carb savory pie.

For the savory pie crust:
- 3/4 cup of almond flour

- 3 tablespoons of coconut flour

- 1/3 cup of sesame seeds

- 3 tablespoons of olive oil

- 3 to 4 tablespoons of water

- 1 egg large

- 2 teaspoons of instant yeast

- 1/2 teaspoon of salt

For quiche filling:

- 8 oz salmon

- 1/2 cup of whipping cream

- 1/2 cup of shredded cheese

- 1/4 cup of parmesan

- 4 eggs

- 1 chopped small onion

- 1 chopped green onion

- 2 1/2 tablespoons of butter

- 1 1/2 tablespoons of fresh dill or parsley

- 1/4 teaspoon ground black pepper

- 1 teaspoon salt

Instructions:

Follow the method mentioned below to make keto low-carb savory pie.

1. Add all the savory pie crust ingredients to the bread machine container. Select the dough cycle press the start button.

2.When kneading completes, remove dough and spread on the greased pie pan, flatten dough with your fingers and prick holes using a fork in the crust.

3.At 350 F/180 C preheated oven, bake for 15 minutes or until it turns light brown.

4.Once done, allow the crust to cool down. Meanwhile, make salmon quiche filling.

5.On a medium heat pan, sauté onion in butter until it softens.

6.In a separate bowl, add eggs, whipping cream, cheese, pepper, and salt, whisk until well mixed.

7.On baked crust, first spread cooked onion and fresh parsley/dill, .then add salmon and egg mixture on top.

8.Bake again for 35 to 40 minutes.

9.Allow the salmon quiche to cool for 10 minutes before serving.

10.Serve with fresh cream or salad.

3.10 Keto Fathead Stuffed Pizza Buns

Total time of cooking
1 hour 30 minutes

Servings
4

Nutrition facts

Calories 443(per serving)

Protein 26g

Total Carbs 10g

Fat 34g

Fiber 2g

Ingredients:

Here is the list of ingredients required to make keto fathead stuffed pizza buns.

For fathead dough:

- 1 1/2 cups of shredded mozzarella (melted)

- 3 eggs (1 for egg wash,2 for dough)

- 3/4 cup of almond flour

- 5 tablespoons of cream cheese (melted)

- 2 teaspoons of instant yeast

- 2 teaspoons of xanthan gum

- pinch of salt

For the stuffed filling:

- 1/4 cup cheddar or mozzarella cheese

- 4 tablespoons of cooked Italian sausage

- 8 slices of pepperoni

- 2 tablespoons of feta cheese

For garnishing:

- 1/4 cup of shredded parmesan

- 1 tablespoon of butter

- 1 teaspoon of Italian seasoning

Instructions:

Follow the method mentioned below to make keto fathead pizza buns.

1.Assemble all the ingredients.

2.In the bread machine container, add all the ingredients of fathead pizza dough in the order suggested by your bread machine: select dough cycle and press start. During kneading, checks dough consistency if required, add two tablespoons of water.

3.When the machine beeps, remove dough from the pan and knead with wet hands for few minutes. Divide the dough into four equal balls.

4.Flatten all four dough balls with a rolling pin, fill in the stuffed filling ingredients in the center of each ball and close the ball with your hands.

5.Brush each ball with egg wash, place stuffed pizza buns on a non-stick baking sheet and bake for 25 to 30 minutes on the middle rack of the oven at 350 F/180 C.

6.Mix Italian seasoning with melted butter and brush over the top of each bun. Sprinkle parmesan cheese over the pizza buns and serve.

3.11 Keto Onion And Cheese Bread Low Carb

Total time of cooking
3 hour 10 minutes

Servings
23

Nutrition facts
Calories 75(per serving)

Protein 7.5g

Net Carbs 1.5g

Fat 7g

Fiber 1g

Ingredients:
Here is the list of ingredients required to make keto onion and cheese bread.

- 2 cups of almond flour
- 1.5 cups of shredded cheese
- 1/4 cup of chopped green onions
- 1 cup of water
- 1/4 cup of sour cream
- 1/2 chopped small onion
- 4 scoops of unflavored whey powder
- 1 chopped shallot
- 3 minced garlic cloves
- 2 teaspoon of instant yeast
- 1 teaspoon of chili flakes
- 1 teaspoon of xanthan gum
- 1/2 teaspoon of salt
- 1/2 teaspoon of pepper

Instructions:

Follow the method mentioned below to make keto onion and cheese bread.

1.Put all the onion and cheese bread ingredients into the bread machine pan in the order suggested by your bread maker. Do not add onions and shallot Close down the lid of the machine, select simple bread settings and choose medium crust, and start the machine.

2.When the machine beeps for extra ingredients, add onions and shallot.

3.When done, remove baked bread from the pan and let it cool down.

4.Once cooled, cut into slices and enjoy.

3.12 Keto Pesto Chicken Cheese Pizza

Total time of cooking
1 hour

Servings
8

Nutrition facts
Calories 387(per slice)

Protein 27.2g

Net Carbs 5.1g

Fat 28.9g

Ingredients:
Here is the list of ingredients required to make keto pesto chicken cheese pizza.

- 1 1/2 cups of almond flour
- 1 egg
- 3 1/2 cups of shredded mozzarella
- 2 tablespoons of olive oil
- 2 to 3 tablespoons of water
- 1 1/2 teaspoons of dry yeast
- 1 teaspoon of xanthan gum
- 1 teaspoon of salt

For topping:
- 3/4 cup of shredded chicken
- 1/2 cups of shredded mozzarella
- 6 cherry tomatoes
- 3 tablespoons of pesto

- 2 tablespoons of sliced roasted bell pepper
- 1 1/2 tablespoons of keto garlic sauce
- 4 oz sliced mozzarella

Instructions:
Follow the method mentioned below to make keto pesto chicken cheese pizza.

1.Meltdown 3 1/2 cups of mozzarella cheese in a microwave oven.

2.Place water, olive oil, egg, mozzarella cheese, almond flour, xanthan gum, salt, and yeast on top of dry ingredients into the machine pan.

3.Pick dough cycle from settings and start the machine.

4.When the kneading procedure is done, remove it from the machine, roll it out with a rolling pin, and spread it into greased pizza sheet.

5.Cover the pizza pan and leave it for 25 minutes to rise.

6.Spread pesto and garlic sauce evenly on the top of the pizza crust.

7.Top up with chicken, tomatoes, bell pepper, shredded cheese, and sliced mozzarella.

8.Bake for 20 minutes at 380 F preheated oven until the crust turns golden brown, and cheese melts down.

9.Make eight slices with a pizza cutter and serve.

3.13 Classic Keto Baguette With Garlic Butter

Total time of cooking
1 hour 50 minutes

Servings
32

Nutrition facts
Calories 27(For 2 baguettes, per serving)

Protein 1.2g

Net Carbs 0.4g

Total Fat 1.4g

Ingredients:
Here is the list of ingredients required to make a classic keto baguette with garlic butter.

For Baguettes dough:
- 1 cup hot water

- 3/4 cup of coconut flour

- 3/4 cup of golden flaxseed (make a powder using seeds grinder)

- 6 large egg whites

- 3 tablespoons of apple cider vinegar

- 3 tablespoons of psyllium husk

- 2 teaspoons of instant yeast

- 1/2 teaspoon of salt

For the garlic butter:
- 1/2 cup of softened butter

- 1/4 cup of any cheese of your choice

- 4 tablespoons of minced garlic

- 1 1/2 teaspoon of parsley

(Mix them all in a bowl)

Instructions:
Follow the method mentioned below to make a keto baguette.

1.Gather all the ingredients.

2.Place all the ingredients for the baguette in the bread machine container, start the machine and choose the dough cycle.

3.Once done, place your dough into a floured surface and knead for few minutes, divide into two portions and make two 9" inches long dough.

4.On the baking sheet, place both doughs. Mark diagonal cuts on the top of the dough.

5.For about 45 to 50 minutes, bake at 350 F/180 C preheated oven.

6.Place baguettes on the wire rack for cooling.

7.Cut each baguette into slices and spread garlic bread before serving.

8.Enjoy

3.14 Tasty Cheese And Garlic Pull-Apart Keto Bread

Total time of cooking
1 hour 25 minutes

Servings
10

Nutrition facts
Calories 302(per serving)

Protein 16g

Carbs 6g

Fat 10g

Fiber 3g

Ingredients:
Here is the list of ingredients required to make cheese and garlic pull-apart bread.

- 1 1/3 cups of almond flour

- 3 cups of grated mozzarella cheese

- 1 cup of grated cheddar cheese

- 1/4 cups of sliced green onion

- 2 medium-sized eggs

- 2 garlic cloves

- 4 tablespoons of salted butter

- 2 tablespoons of warm water

- 2 tablespoons of chives

- 2 teaspoons of dried yeast

- 2 teaspoons of inulin

- 2 teaspoons of xanthan gum

- 1 teaspoon of salt

- pinch of pepper

Instructions:
Follow the method mentioned below to make cheese and garlic pull-apart bread.

1.In a microwave-safe bowl, mix cheese and butter until completely melts.

2.Combine inulin, yeast, and warm water in a bread machine container, leave it for 15 to 20 minutes and let it proof.

3.Now, on top of the yeast mixture, add almond flour, salt, xanthan gum, pour eggs followed by melted cheese and butter mixture, choose dough cycle and start the machine.

4.Once kneading is over. Transfer the dough into a bowl and cover with a kitchen cloth to rise for 20 minutes.

5.Knead the dough with hands for a while, roll out into a rectangular shape on the floured surface.

6.Spread over the cheddar, cheese, garlic, green onions, chive, salt, and pepper.

7.Make a large scroll , rolling the dough from one end to the other.

8.Slit the dough at an angle(approx 3/4 of the way through) with kitchen scissors. Twist each portion of the dough oppositely from the previous one. To overlap the portions and form more of an oval shape. Press the dough together.

9.Place at the greased non-stick baking sheet and leave for 20 minutes.

10.Bake your pull-apart bread for 25 to 30 minutes at 350 F/180 C preheated oven.

11.Allow cooling first for 10 to 15 minutes.

12.Serve on a platter and enjoy.

3.15 Low Carb Keto Spinach Bread

Total time of cooking
3 hour 5 minutes

Servings
8

Nutrition facts
Calories 345(per serving)

Protein 13g

Carbs 7g

Fat 31g

Fiber 4g

Ingredients:
Here is the list of ingredients required to make spinach bread.
- 1 3/4 cups of almond flour

- 1 cup of cheddar cheese

- 1 cup of spinach finely chopped

- 2 eggs large

- 7 tablespoons of melted butter
- 1 tablespoon of rosemary chopped
- 2 clove of garlic finely chopped
- 2 teaspoons of instant yeast
- 1/2 teaspoon of salt

Instructions:

Follow the method mentioned below to make spinach bread.

1.Combine all the ingredients.

2.Put all the ingredients except spinach into your bread maker in the order recommended by your bread machine.

3.Pick bread cycle and medium crust from your bread maker settings panel and start the machine.

4.Check after 5 minutes of kneading. Add two tablespoons of water if needed.

5.At nut signals, add spinach to the mixture.

6.When the bread cycle completes, Remove and allow to cool down for a while.

7.Slice and serve.

3.16 Keto Mexican Jalapeno Cornbread

Total time of cooking
1 hour 15 minutes

Servings
8

Nutrition facts
Calories 412(per serving)

Protein 13g

Carbs 6g

Fat 40g

Fiber 3g

Ingredients:
Here is the list of ingredients for Mexican jalapeno cornbread.

- 2 cups of almond flour

- 1 cup of grated cheddar cheese

- 1 cup of heavy cream

- 1/4 cup of melted butter

- 4 large beaten eggs

- 3 tablespoons of diced jalapenos
- 1 teaspoon of instant yeast
- 1/2 teaspoon of salt

Instructions:
Follow the method mentioned below to make Mexican jalapeno cornbread.

1.Assemble all the ingredients.

2.In the bread maker pan, add all the ingredients except jalapenos, select dough cycle, and start the machine. Check after few minutes if needed, add two tablespoons of water.

3.When the machine beeps five minutes before the last kneading, add jalapenos.

4.Warm up your oven at 350 F.

5.Spray 8 inches oven-safe iron skillet.

6.Place your dough batter into an iron skillet and bake for around 30 minutes.

7.Remove from oven once done, cut in 8 slices, and serve.

Conclusion

The bread machine is such a blessing in the shape of an appliance to get your hands on. The more you play with it and bake new things, the more you can create magic with it and never want to get away with the feeling of how it saves your time and energy and why you always want one in your kitchen.

Practice makes things perfect, so do not hesitate to experiment. You may not master the art of making bread and using a bread machine in just one day. However, you can kick start your learning journey with ample bread recipes combined in this cookbook. Regardless of your expertise in making different kinds of bread and operating a bread machine. Buying and starting with a cookbook will reveal a world of new recipes to you.

Vegan Keto Meal Plan Cookbook with Pictures

The Low-Fat Plan To Burn Fat, Boost Your Energy, Crush Cravings, And Calm Inflammation

By

Jamie Carter

Table of Contents

Introduction

The Ketogenic diet is a low-carb, high-fat, moderate-protein diet marketed for its effective influence on weight loss and general health.

While sometimes connected with animal foods, this form of consumption may be modified to suit plant-based diet plans, like the vegan diet.

All animal products are excluded from vegan diets, rendering low-carb consumption more complicated. However, vegans will enjoy the possible advantages of a Ketogenic diet with proper preparation.

What is the Keto vegan diet?

The Ketogenic diet has a high-fat content, low carbohydrate content, and mild protein content. In order to achieve and sustain ketosis, carbohydrates are usually limited to 20g to 50g a day. Ketosis is a metabolic mechanism in which the body will burn fat for energy instead of glucose.

Because this form of eating contains mainly fat, typically around 75% of the intake, keto dieters also switch to high-fat animal items, such as butter, pork, chicken beef, and all-dairy products.

Many who consume diets focused on vegetables, like vegans, can also adopt a ketogenic diet. Vegan people only eat plant-based products such as fruit, vegetables, and cereals, while avoiding poultry, meat, milk and eggs from animals. By depending on high-fat, plant-based items such as coconut oil, avocados, seeds and nuts, vegans can achieve ketosis.

Vegan Keto Diet Benefits

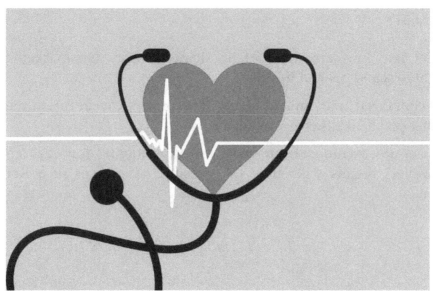

A Vegan Keto diet promises a wide variety of health advantages. A high-fat diet and low-carb are used in the Ketogenic diet. Pairing it with a purely vegan diet allows reduced consumption of carbs and sugar and enhances the absorption of nutrients, which inevitably contributes to outstanding long-term wellbeing. Vegans can achieve ketosis by eating plant-based goods high in healthy fats such as avocados, almonds, seeds, olives and nuts.

So what precisely are the effects of a vegan keto diet for health? How can your physical wellbeing benefit from following this diet?

1. Reduces the likelihood of heart disease

Heart disease is particularly the main culprit of so many deaths globally. Many health problems may cause it, but it is mostly attributed to poor diet, absence of exercise, and obesity.

Many individuals believe that the heart cannot stay healthy with a high-fat diet. But latest findings have shown that healthy fat consumption is safe and offers long-term medical benefits. A regular Vegan Keto diet doesn't really display any substantial rise in cardiac consequences, but it even decreases the extent of heart disease-related fat molecules, triglycerides, flowing in your blood circulation.

2. Preventing and Treating Diabetes and Obesity

The ketogenic diet is a successful way to decrease medication in patients with diabetes, based on research. Because the keto-vegan diet decreases the consumption of carbs and guarantees a diet free of sugar, it reduces sugar levels, which greatly reduces the likelihood of potential diabetes. For the people who have diabetes already, this diet enables them to reduce insulin doses or totally eliminates the drugs in as little as a few weeks. In fact, eating a plant-based diet that is sugar-free and low-carb is an efficient way to lose and manage the target weight.3.

3. Battles some kinds of cancer

Most evidence reveals that sugar fuels cancer cells. Keto-vegan food removes sugar from the system. Your system's reduction in sugars and nutrients starves the cancer cells. A relatively low-carbohydrate diet, for example, can decrease the relapse of some forms of breast cancer. It has even been shown to slow down brain tumor development. Cancerous cells can be deliberately starved by reducing the intake of sugary fruits and starchy vegetables. Many Keto-vegan products help inhibit the growth of cancer cells.

4. Enhances mental health

Researchers believe that a healthy Keto-vegan diet increases mental cognition, strengthening your critical reasoning ability and making you more concentrated. This lifestyle leaves the brain sharp and fresh.

The keto-vegan diet also aims to clear up beta-amyloid cholesterol, which can bind together to block signals from flowing quickly and efficiently in the brain. Preventing this build-up implies reducing the risk of contracting neurodegenerative disorders such as Alzheimer's.

5. Provides good health for the gut and stomach

Having keto-vegan foods in your diet helps your gut to be healthy with a diverse and balanced intestinal microbiome. A strong gut with lots of beneficial bacteria allows the body to consume nutrients and fats more easily and more safely. These healthy bacteria benefit you by having a strong lining of the intestine that helps break down your food and promotes the absorption of nutrients. Some bacteria in the intestine also help to supply your body with vitamins B12 and potassium that are necessary for regulating minerals such as calcium in your body. Besides, this diet makes sure the metabolism is balanced.

6. Helps to improve eye and vision

It is possible to avoid glaucoma and cataracts, chronic conditions that cause blurred vision or perhaps even blindness, with a keto-vegan lifestyle. Getting a diet that is low in carbs but high in healthy fats will improve the health of the retinal cells and reduce cell degeneration as well.

7. Hormones Stabilizes

In the body, hormones are molecular messengers. There may be chaotic hormonal imbalances. Ketosis has a positive effect on hormones. It reduces the body's insulin levels by eliminating sugar from the diet. Other than that, leptin levels, a form of hormones that suppresses appetite, are lowered, allowing you to manage your eating behaviors.

In women following the Keto-vegan diet, their pituitary gland performs much better, controlling progesterone and thyroid to reduce infertility and progesterone deficiency.

8. Clearer and cleaner skin

In your system, reducing carbohydrates results in cleaner skin. Simple carbs and dairy products can also cause inflammation, which is one of the main causes of acne.

High-glycemic food can make acne worse and also cause breakouts. Although sugar and carbohydrates are known to induce pimples, healthy fats can alleviate dry skin and inhibit inflammatory acne from occurring. So, if you desire your skin to be smoother, clearer and brighter, this diet is the answer.

9. Provides greater amounts of vitality to assist you in getting around during the day

Increased carb consumption makes you feel sluggish. The starches found in the foods are converted into glucose as you eat food rich in carbohydrates (pizza, for example). There would be an increase in energy after eating extra carbs, but a major decline will come immediately, leaving you to feel slow and exhausted after having a meal.

You will face none of these difficulties on a Keto vegan diet. Instead of carbs, your body would then depend on fats. It would not need energy from carbohydrates. Increased insulin production can be stopped, and at any moment, the body will now use fat reserves. You will experience a steady supply of energy during the day with this.

10. Helps improve sleep

Also, it enhances sleep. The best thing about complying with this plan's that it lets you stay up and about in the daytime and gives you a satisfying, nice night's sleep.

Sleep cycles change thanks to a decrease in carbohydrates and a rise in healthy fats. Researchers believe that a vegan- keto diet could influence the development of a chemical in the brain, adenosine, which controls sleep.

Besides weight loss, the Vegan-keto diet has so many health benefits. It would be a long list if we started to mention them all in here. Try a keto-vegan program now and enjoy all the wellness benefits that it will bring!

Foods to avoid on a vegan keto diet

When ensuing to a keto vegan diet, you must considerably decrease your carb consumption and substitute carbs with healthy fats and vegan protein sources.to

Animal products, including meat, poultry, dairy eggs, and seafood, are omitted from a keto vegan diet.

These are some of the foods that must be completely shunned:

Seafood: Fish, clams, shrimp, mussels.

Meat and poultry: Turkey, chicken, pork beef.

Eggs: Egg whites and yolks.

Animal-based products: Honey, whey protein, egg white protein.

Dairy: Milk, yogurt, butter.

These foods ought to be considerably reduced:

Sugary drinks: Soda, juice, sweet tea, sports drinks, chocolate milk smoothies.

Alcoholic beverages, high in carbs, wine, sweetened cocktails, beer.

Diet foods Low in fat: Low-fat products tend to be elevated in added sugar.

Grains and starches: Cereal, bread, baked goods, rice, grains, pasta.

Legumes and Beans: Red kidney beans, black and white chickpeas and black beans.

Sweeteners: Maple syrup, white sugar, Brown sugar, agave.

Starchy vegetables: Sweet potatoes, winter squash, potatoes, peas beets.

Fruits: Limit all fruit intake. Nevertheless, few fruits like different berries are permitted in small portions.

Processed foods: Restrain from packaged foods and encourage consumption of whole, unrefined foods.

High-carb sauces and condiments: Marinades, sweetened salad dressings, Barbecue sauce,

The degree of carbohydrate limitation when doing a keto vegan plan differs depending upon the individual's requirements and health objectives.

In general, vegan protein sources and Good, high-fat vegan foods should be prevalent in your diet.

Foods to consume on a keto vegan diet

Following a healthy keto vegan diet requires that the vegan meals be made of low-carb and high-fat.

In the keto vegan diet, some permissible foods are:

Oils: MCT oil, olive oil, coconut oil, nut oil, avocado oil.

Coconut produces: Unsweetened coconut (flakes or shredded), coconut cream, Full-fat coconut milk.

Non-starchy veggies: Brussels sprouts, zucchini Leafy greens, broccoli, cauliflower, mushrooms peppers.

Nuts and seeds: Hemp seeds, walnuts, almonds, Brazil nuts, macadamia nuts, pumpkin seeds, chia seeds.

Seed and nut butter: Butters from sunflower seeds, almonds, cashews, peanuts.

Vegan "dairy": Vegan cream cheese, full-fat coconut yogurt, vegan butter, cashew cheese.

Vegan sources of protein: Tempeh, tofu (full-fat).

Berries: Raspberries Blueberries, strawberries and blackberries, can be consumed in control.

Avocados: Guacamole Whole avocados.

Condiments: Fresh herbs, spices, nutritional yeast, lemon juice, pepper, salt,

Since the keto diet leaves out several of the food types that vegans depend on, such as starchy veggies and whole grains, the keto vegan diet can indeed be adopted adequately.

Drawbacks and side effects

Although the vegan keto diet may be helpful to your wellbeing, it has some possible drawbacks.

Downsides

Keto vegan diets appear to be low in essential nutrients, — particularly if not carefully prepared. Vitamin D, vitamin K2, vitamin B12, omega-3 fats, zinc, iron and calcium, are some of the nutrients deficient in some vegan diets.

The Vegan Keto diet has more limitations than any normal vegan diet; that's why it is necessary to be fortified with high-quality vitamins and minerals. The meals you prepare should guarantee that you are consuming a nutritionally balanced diet.

Consuming fortified foods, concentrating on whole foods, and consuming nutrients, such as fermentation and sprouts, is vital for individuals adopting a vegan keto diet.

However, it can be difficult for individuals on the vegan keto diet to fulfill their micro-nutrient needs with the vegan or keto foods alone. Supplementing some minerals and vitamins that are typically deficient in vegan diets is a clever way to reduce future shortages and guarantee that your everyday requirements are fulfilled.

Adverse Effects

It may be daunting to switch to a ketogenic diet.

Sometimes termed keto flu, the body may find it difficult to move from a higher carbohydrate diet to a keto diet.

When your body changes from using glucose to fat for energy, painful symptoms can occur.

Adverse effects of vegan keto diets may include:

- Headaches
- Diarrhea
- Fatigue
- Irritability
- Nausea
- Poor concentration

- Muscle cramps
- Weakness
- Difficulty sleeping
- Constipation
- Dizziness

Drinking plenty of water, having adequate rest, consuming fiber-rich meals and participating in moderate exercise will help relieve keto-flu effects.

Also, potassium, magnesium, and sodium electrolyte supplementation may help alleviate some effects, such as muscle pain, fatigue and insomnia.

Since the vegan keto diet limits certain items, it is not appropriate for all.

A vegan keto diet might not be appropriate for people with diabetes, type 1 ladies who are breast-feeding or are pregnant, sports professionals or those with a history of disordered eating.

When you are considering a transition to a keto vegan diet, contact a doctor or a licensed health provider first to confirm that your diet is healthy to adopt.

Chapter 1- Breakfast

1. Vegan Scrambled Eggs

Prep. Time: 10 minutes

Cook Time: 10 minutes

Servings: 4

Serving size: ¼ of the recipe

Nutrition as per serving

182 kcal/ 11g fat / 8g carbs / 14g protein / 2g fiber = 6g net carbs

Ingredients

- Silken tofu 300 g
- Plant-based milk, unsweetened   ½ cup
- Nutritional yeast 2 tbsp.
- Almond flour 2 tbsp.
- Ground turmeric heaped ¼ tsp.
- Dijon mustard 1 tsp.
- Cornstarch or cornflour 2 tsp.
- Indian black salt 1 tsp.+ more to taste
- Fine salt ½ tsp. + more to taste
- Black pepper ½ tsp. + more to taste
- Onion powder ½ tsp.
- Garlic powder ½ tsp.
- Vegan butter 2 tbsp.
- Extra-firm or firm tofu 350 g (for crumbling effect to get eggy texture)

Directions

1. In a blender, add the milk, silken tofu, nutritional yeast, turmeric, almond flour, mustard, pepper, cornstarch, black salt, salt, garlic powder, onion powder, and blend absolutely smooth.
2. Crush the other chunk of tofu, either with fingers or use a potato masher.
3. In a large frypan, melt the vegan butter over a medium-low flame. When it melts, add the crushed tofu. Cook it for a couple of minutes, then add in the smoothly blended tofu mixture. Stir and continue occasionally stirring until the desired texture is reached for about 5 minutes. It should be slightly runny and silky. It will get drier if you cook longer. Once you take it off the heat, it will keep cooking a little so keep that in mind.
4. When ready, taste the seasoning and add black salt, salt, and pepper if necessary and serve immediately.

2. Avocado & Vegan Bulletproof Coffee

Prep. Time: 5 minutes

Servings: 1

Serving size 1 vegan Bpc + half avocado

Nutrition as per serving

255 kcal / 26g fat / 7g carbs / 1g protein /5g fiber = 2g net carb

Ingredients

- Coffee 1 cup
- Cinnamon a pinch
- MCT oil 1 tbsp.
- Avocado ½
- For Everything Bagel Seasoning:
- White sesame seeds 2 tbsp.
- Garlic dried minced 1 tbsp.
- Coarse sea salt, 1 tbsp.
- Poppy seeds 1 tbsp.
- Onion dried minced 1 tbsp.
- Black sesame seeds 1 tbsp.

Directions

1. Add MCT oil, brewed coffee, and cinnamon in a blender, process until frothy, then transfer to a coffee mug to serve.
2. Mix all seasoning ingredients in a bowl.
3. Cut avocado into half, remove skin and slice as preferred.
4. Sprinkle the prepared seasoning. Serve!

3. Overnight Vegan Keto Chia Pudding

Prep. Time: 10 minutes

Resting time: 6 hours

Servings: 1

Serving size: 1 bowl

Nutrition as per serving

151 kcal / 10g fat / 12.5g carbs / 11g fiber / 5g protein = 1.5g net carbs

Ingredients

For the keto chia pudding

- Plant-based milk (e.g., almond, coconut, or macadamia)1 cup
- Chia seeds, 3 tbsp.
- Keto liquid sweetener (e.g., vanilla stevia drops.) To taste
- Preferred toppings -optional

Directions

1. Add chia seeds to the milk mixing thoroughly, cover and chill in the refrigerator overnight.
2. If it is not of desired consistency, add more liquid. Add keto Sweetener to taste and sprinkle desired toppings and serve.

3. Store in a sealed container in the refrigerator for up to 5 days (i.e., it's perfect for meal prepping!).

4. Low Carb Keto Oatmeal

Prep. Time: 1 minute

Cook Time: 4 minute

Servings: 1 serving

Serving size: 1 bowl

Nutrition as per serving

250kcal / 17g fat /16g carbs / 15g fiber / 8g protein = 1g net carbs

Ingredients

- Coconut milk, unsweetened, cold 1/2 cup
- Water, hot 1/2 cup
- 2 tbsp. each of
- Unsweetened shredded coconut
- Ground flaxseed
- Granulated sweetener, keto-friendly
- Chia seeds

Directions

1. Add the dry ingredients to a small mixing container, and mix well.
2. Pour the hot water into the dry ingredients and mix well; it will turn out super thick. Pour in the cold coconut milk and whisk until it becomes creamy and thick 'oatmeal.'
3. Sprinkle mix-ins or toppings of choice and serve.

5. Tofu Shakshuka

Prep. Time: 5 minutes

Cook Time: 20 minutes

Servings: 2

Serving size: Half the recipe

Nutrition as per serving

284kcal / 9.4g fat / 26.6g carbs / 9.2g fiber / 20.3g protein = 16 net carbs

Ingredients

- Olive oil 1 tablespoon (optional)
- Garlic 4 large cloves
- Tomatoes diced 1 can (750 ml)
- Salt 1 tsp.
- Pepper ½ tsp.
- Dried mixed herbs (or oregano or Italian seasoning) 2 tsp.
- Dried chili flakes 1/2 tsp.
- Medium tofu, unpressed, cut into rounds 1 block (approx.350g)
- Indian black salt optional

Directions

1. In a skillet, heat the olive oil and sauté the garlic on medium heat until it starts to brown a little. (For an oil-free recipe: use a tbsp. of water as a replacement for the oil).
2. Include the tomatoes, pepper, salt, herbs, and chili flakes.
3. Simmer for 5 minutes on medium heat, then put in the tofu rounds.
4. Decrease the heat and simmer on medium-low for 15 minutes till the tofu is soft, and the sauce starts to thicken up a little and thoroughly heated.
5. Add Indian Black Salt just before serving.
6. Serve with keto toast, if your macros allow!

6. Vegan Keto Protein Smoothie Bowl

Prep. Time: 5 minutes

Servings: 1

Serving size: 1 smoothie bowl

Nutrition as per serving

615 kcal / 54g fat / 19g carbs / 13g fiber / 23g protein = 6g net carbs

Ingredients

For Green Smoothie Bowl:

- Spinach 1 cup
- Almond milk unsweetened 2–3 Tbsp.
- Avocado ½
- Macadamia nut butter 1 Tbsp.
- Plain almond milk yogurt, unsweetened ⅔ cup
- Keto sweetener, to taste
- Spirulina powder 2 tsp.

For Toppings:

- Hemp hearts 1 Tbsp.
- Pumpkin seeds 2 Tbsp.
- Chia seeds 1 Tbsp.

Directions

1. Place all the smoothie ingredients (excluding toppings) into a blender and mix until smooth. Add sweetener to taste, altering thickness to preference.
2. Transfer to a bowl, sprinkle on the toppings, and serve!

For meal prep:

1. Keep avocado, spinach, spirulina and nut butter in a freezer-safe bag or jar and freeze.
2. To prepare, before placing in the blender, thaw slightly add milk and yogurt.
3. Blend, pour in a bowl serve with toppings!

7. Cauliflower and Greens Smoothie Bowl

Prep. Time: 5 minutes

Cook Time: 10 minutes

Servings: 2

Serving size: 1 bowl w/o toppings

Nutrition as per serving

253kcal / 14.8g fat / 18.5g carbs / 7g fiber / 12g protein = 4.2g net carbs

Ingredients

- Cauliflower, frozen 1/2 cup
- Zucchini, frozen 1/2 cup
- Spinach (or kale, for calcium boost), frozen loosely packed1 cup
- Blueberries or blackberries, frozen 1 cup
- Milk alternate 1 cup (try almond-milk or hemp milk or canned coconut milk)
- Peanut butter (or almond butter) 2 tbsp.
- Hemp hearts 3 tbsp.
- Cinnamon ground 1 tsp

Toppings- Optional

- Granola (grain-free for low-carb)
- Berries frozen or fresh
- Hemp hearts

Directions

This recipe goes well with frozen zucchini and cauliflower. Cauliflower can be steamed first, but when using a high-speed blender, it will not be necessary. Frozen spinach as well as fresh works fine.

1. In a high-speed blender, put in all the smoothie ingredients, place the frozen ingredients first. Blend until a smooth consistency is reached and all is well incorporated.
2. Split this banana-free smoothie mixture into two soup bowls. Garnish with additional hemp hearts and homemade granola.

8. Maple Low Carb Oatmeal

Prep. Time: 5 minutes

Cook Time: 20 minutes

Servings: 4 servings

Serving size 1 cup

Nutrition as per serving

374kcal / 34.59g fat /28g carbs / 24.7g fiber / 9.25g protein = 3.27g net carbs

Ingredients

- Unsweetened almond milk 4 cups
- Walnuts 1/2 cups
- Sunflower seeds 1/4 cups
- Pecans 1/2 cups
- Coconut flakes 1/4 cup
- Chia seeds 4 tbsp.
- Stevia powder 3/8 tsp
- Cinnamon 1/2 tsp
- Maple flavoring 1 tsp (optional)

Directions

1. In a food processor, place the pecans, walnuts, sunflower seeds, and pulse to have them coarsely chopped.
2. Place all the ingredients in a large saucepan and heat on low. Keep simmering for about 20 to 30 minutes, occasionally stirring, until most of the liquid has been absorbed by the chia seeds. Keep stirring, so the seeds don't stick to the saucepan at the bottom.
3. Once the oatmeal thickens, take off from heat and serve while hot. It can also be cooled down and stored in the refrigerator for the next day's breakfast.

4.

Chapter 2- Lunch

1. Low Carb Vegan Tahini Bowl

Prep. Time: 10 minutes

Cook Time: 35 minutes

Servings: 1

Serving size: 1 bowl

Nutrition as per serving

641 Kcal / 5g fat / 33g carbs / 20g fiber / 23g protein = 13g net carbs

Ingredients

For Vegetable Bowl:

- Brussels sprouts 1 cup
- Broccoli florets 1½ cups
- Tahini 2 Tbsp.
- Pumpkin seeds 2 Tbsp.
- Kalamata olives 10
- Oil ½ tsp
- Salt a pinch
- Avocado, ½ for serving
- Sesame seeds sprinkle for topping

Directions

1. Heat the oven to 220°C (425°F).
2. Line a pan with foil or parchment and add Brussels sprouts, broccoli, and pumpkin seeds. Add tahini, oil, salt and mix.

3. Roast for 35 minutes.
4. Take out from the oven, place Kalamata olives to veggies in the pan, and toss to mix.
5. Transfer to a bowl top with half sliced avocado, then sprinkle some sesame seeds!

2. Easy Low Carb Creamy Spinach

Prep. Time: 5 minutes

Cook Time: 10 minutes

Servings: 4

Serving size: 1/2 cup

Nutrition as per serving

274kcal / 27g fat / 5 g carbs / 1g fiber / 4g protein = 4 net carbs

Ingredients

- Butter 3 tbsp.
- Baby spinach chopped 16 cups (10 oz.)
- Cream cheese, chopped 3 oz.
- Heavy cream 1/2 cup
- Italian seasoning1 tsp.
- Garlic, minced 4 cloves
- Black pepper 1/4 tsp.
- Sea salt 1/4 tsp.
- Parmesan cheese, for topping (optional)

Directions

1. In a large wok or a sauté pan, heat butter over medium heat. Add in minced garlic and fry until fragrant.
2. Include spinach. Fry for 3 to 5 minutes until wilted. Cover the pan if it is too full of stirring at first. Covering it for a few minutes will wilt the spinach quickly. Then cook, stirring until the spinach is almost dry.
3. Add cream cheese, heavy cream, Italian seasoning, black pepper, and sea salt. Stir continuously until the cheese has melted, then cook for 3-4 minutes until thickened.
4. If preferred, sprinkle with Parmesan cheese before serving.

3. Mashed Cauliflower with Garlic and Herbs

Prep. Time: 10 minutes

Cook Time: 10 minutes

Servings: 4

Serving size: ¼ of the recipe

Nutrition as per serving

84.6kcal / 4g fat / 10.9g carbs / 4g fiber / 4.1g protein = 6.9g net carbs

Ingredients

- Cauliflower 1 head
- Olive oil 1 tbsp.
- Garlic, minced 2 cloves
- Herbs chopped finely (rosemary, thyme, parsley, sage, chives, etc.) 1-2 tsp

Directions

1. Trim off the leaves from the cauliflower and remove the florets. Wash the florets.
2. In a pot, heat water (about 1-inch) on medium heat. When the water started boiling, place a steamer insert inside the pot and placed the cauliflower florets in it. Steam for about 6-8 minutes.
3. In the meantime, take a small pan and heat the olive oil on medium heat. Put in the minced garlic, then cook for 30 seconds, and take off the heat.
4. Take out the steamer insert, discard the water, and then add the steamed cauliflower back into the pot. Add the garlic, olive oil, and chopped herbs.
5. Use a stick blender or a potato to gently mix all the ingredients with the cauliflower, do not puree. Serve immediately.

4. Keto Mac and Cheese with Vegan Cheese Sauce

Prep. Time: 5 minutes

Cook Time: 20 minutes

Servings: 4

Serving size: 1 cup

Nutrition as per serving

294kcal / 23g fat / 12g carbs / 5g fiber / 11g protein = 7g net carbs

Ingredients

- Cauliflower (cut into small florets) 1 head
- Butter 2 tbsp. + 1 tbsp.
- Sea salt
- Black pepper
- For the cheese sauce
- Hemp seeds hulled 1 cup
- Nutritional yeast 1/2 cup
- Bell pepper chopped (red, orange or yellow) 1/4 cup
- Salt 1 tsp.
- Onion Powder 1/2 tsp.
- Garlic powder 1/2 tsp.
- water ½ -1 cup

Directions

1. Heat the oven to 232 degrees c (450 degrees f). Line foil or parchment paper on a baking tray.
2. Melt 2 tbsp. of butter in the microwave. In a large mixing bowl, mix the cauliflower florets and the melted butter together. Add black pepper and sea salt to taste.
3. Assemble the seasoned cauliflower florets on the lined baking tray. Bake for about 10 to 15 minutes, or until crispy and tender.
4. Prepare the sauce: Put all ingredients in a blender with half a cup of water in at first and blend until smooth for about 2 minutes. Then gradually add the rest until a thick cheesy consistency is reached. You may need less quantity of water!
5. Mix the cauliflower in the cheese sauce and bake for about 20 minutes just before serving.

5. Indian Masala Whole Roasted Cauliflower in Instant Pot

Prep. Time: 5 minutes

Cook Time: 5 minutes

Servings: 8 servings

Serving size: 1/8 of the recipe

Nutrition as per serving

161 kcal / 10g fat / 16g carbs / 6g fiber / 5g protein = 10g net carbs

Ingredients

- Cauliflower 1 whole head
- Onions, diced 2 large
- Tomatoes, diced 5
- Cashews, ½ cup (soaked in almond milk ½ cup)
- Ginger chopped 1 tsp

- Garlic chopped 1 tsp
- Oil 2 tbsp.
- Cumin seeds ½ tsp
- Black cardamoms 2
- Green cardamom 1
- Cloves 3
- Peppercorn 4
- Bay leaf 1
- Turmeric powder ½ tsp
- Coriander powder 1 tsp
- Red chilly powder 1 tsp (optional)
- Garam masala ½ tsp
- Cilantro, chopped 1 tbsp.
- Roasted sesame seeds 1 tsp (optional)
- Water 2 cups
- Salt to taste

Directions

1. Heat the Instant Pot mode to "Sauté." Put in oil, cloves, cumin seeds, black cardamoms, peppercorns, bay leaf and green cardamom. Stir.
2. Include onions, garlic, ginger and salt. Cook till onions are transparent.
3. At this point, add in the spices, turmeric, chili powder, and coriander powder. Cook for about 2 minutes more, stirring occasionally.
4. Put in the coarsely chopped tomatoes and stir well. Keep cooking until the oil begins to separate. Discard the black cardamoms and bay leaf.
5. In a blender, add cashews and milk, blend slowly, adding hot water. It should be a smooth paste and add it to the instant pot.
6. Now remove the bottom of the cauliflower and wash thoroughly.
7. Add a cup of water and the trivet to the Instant Pot.
8. Position Instant Pot for 00:00 minutes to High "Pressure." Seal the valve. Once the timer is off, move the valve to Vent for Quick release of the pressure.
9. Open the Instant Pot and let the cauliflower cool down a little.
10. Transfer the cauliflower to a serving dish and add half of the sauce.
11. Optional- broil the sauce-covered cauliflower for a few minutes.
12. Sprinkle garam masala cilantro and roasted sesame seeds on top and serve.

6. Low Carb Vegetable Soup

Prep. Time: 5 minutes

Cook Time: 30 minutes

Servings: 12

Serving size: 1 cup

Nutrition as per serving

79kcal / 2g fat / 11g carbs / 3g fiber / 2g protein = 8g net carbs

Ingredients

- Vegetable broth 8 cups
- Olive oil 2 tbsp.
- Bell peppers, chopped, 2 large
- Garlic, minced 4 cloves
- Onion, chopped 1 large
- Cauliflower, 1-inch florets 1 medium head
- Diced tomatoes 2 cans (14.5-oz each)
- Green beans, cleaned 1-inch pieces 2 cups
- Italian seasoning 1 tbsp.
- Bay leaves dried 2 (optional)
- Black pepper, to taste (optional)
- Sea salt to taste, (optional)

Directions

1. In a pot, heat the olive oil on medium heat
2. Include the bell peppers and onions. Fry for 7 to 10 minutes till onions are just starting to brown.
3. Include the minced garlic and fry until fragrant for 1 minute.
4. Add the broth, green beans, cauliflower, Italian seasoning and diced tomatoes. Season with black pepper and sea salt to taste. Put in the bay leaves. Take it to a boil on high heat, decrease the heat to medium-low cover, and cook until vegetables are soft for about 12 to 18 minutes.

7. Red Curry Cauliflower Soup

Prep. Time: 15 minutes

Cook Time: 30 minutes

Servings: 8 servings

Serving size: 1cup

Nutrition as per serving

227kcal / 16 g fat / 18g carbs / 7g fiber / 6g protein = 11g net carbs

Ingredients

- Yellow onion, sliced 1 medium
- Garlic sliced 3 medium cloves
- Thai curry paste, red 4 oz. (about 4 tbsp.)

- Cauliflower florets 1 lb.
- Red lentils 1/2 cup
- Water 1 1/2 cups
- Vegetable broth, low-sodium 4 cups
- Himalayan pink salt 1/2 tsp.
- Black pepper 1/2 tsp.
- Coconut milk, unsweetened 1 can (14 oz.)
- Lemon juice 3 tbsp.
- Chives sliced 1 tbsp.

Directions

1. In a large saucepan, heat 3-4 tbsp. vegetable broth with the sliced onions until soft. Include the sliced garlic. Keep cooking for 1 to 2 minutes more until fragrant.
2. Add the cauliflower florets, red curry paste, water, red lentils, salt, black pepper, and 4 cups of vegetable broth into the saucepan. Heat the soup to a slow simmer and then decrease the heat to medium. Keep cooking until the red lentils and cauliflower are tender, stirring once in a while or for 15 to 20 minutes.
3. Pour the soup into a blender jug and completely blend the soup on high until it is smooth.
4. Transfer the blended soup to the saucepan and mix in the coconut milk on medium heat. Stir in the lemon juice and sprinkle chives on top before serving.

8. Thai Zucchini Noodles

Prep. Time: 15 minutes

Servings: 6 cups

Serving size: 1 cup

Nutrition as per serving

216kcal / 14g fat / 9g carbs / 4g fiber / 9g protein = 5g net carbs

Ingredients

- Grape tomatoes halved 1/2 cup
- Carrot julienned or spirals 1 large
- Red cabbage sliced thinly 1/2 cup
- Zucchini - thin or spiral noodles 1
- Thai basil 10 leaves
- For the peanut sauce:
- Garlic minced 1 clove
- Ginger fresh minced 1 tsp.
- Peanut butter creamy low carb 1 tbsp.
- Lime or lemon juice 1 tbsp.
- Soy sauce 1 tbsp.
- Red pepper flakes ¼ tsp.

- Cilantro leaves, peanuts unsalted roasted, and lime wedges for garnishing. (optional)

Directions

1. Whisk together the ginger, garlic, peanut butter, lime or lemon juice, red pepper flakes and soy sauce in a small bowl until well-blended and smooth. Add 1 to 2 tablespoon of water if it seems too thick, and blend.
2. Combine the carrots, zucchini noodles, red cabbage, basil leaves and tomatoes together. Mix in the peanut sauce. Lightly mix all together. Transfer all veggies and noodles to a serving platter.
3. Sprinkle a few peanuts and garnish wedges of lime if preferred. Enjoy!!

9. Creamy Tomato Soup

Prep. Time: 5 minutes

Cook Time: 5 minutes

Servings: 8 servings

Serving size: 1 cup

Nutrition as per serving

60kcal / 2g fat / 9g carbs / 2g fiber / 2g protein = 7g net carbs

Ingredients

- Vegetable broth 3 ½ cups
- Tomatoes with juice 3 cans (15oz)
- Green onions scallions 4
- Minced Garlic 1 tsp.
- Smoked paprika ½ tsp.
- Dried oregano 1 tsp.

- Basil 6 leaves
- Almond butter 2-3 tbsp.-optional
- Black pepper to taste
- Toasted almonds for topping -optional
- Salt to taste

Directions

1. Place all the ingredients in a large pot.
2. Heat to boiling, and decrease the heat to let it simmer till thick for about 20 min.
3. Blend the soup in a blender. Pour into bowls.
4. Sprinkle toasted nuts (if preferred) and serve.

Chapter 3- Dinner

1. Broccoli Fried Rice

Prep. Time: 5 minutes

Cook Time: 3 minutes

Servings: 4 servings

Serving size: 1 bowl

Nutrition as per serving

87kcal / 5g fat / 7g carbs / 4g fiber / 2g protein = 4.2g net carbs

Ingredients

- Broccoli, riced, (approx. 2 heads of broccoli) 4 cups
- Avocado oil 1 tbsp.
- Garlic finely chopped 1 tbsp.
- Coconut amino 1 tbsp.
- Toasted sesame oil 1 ½ tsp.
- Coarse salt ¼ to ½ tsp.
- Ginger grated ¼ - ½ tsp.
- Lime juice 1 tbsp. + more for serving
- Scallions, chopped 2 bulbs

- Parsley or cilantro, chopped 4 tbsp. (optional)
- Almonds sliced (optional)

Optional pairings:

- Shrimp, medium size, peeled & uncooked ½ lb.
- Fresh scallops 8-10
- Black pepper ⅛ tsp.
- Coarse salt ¼ tsp.

Directions

1. Heat a skillet to high, add olive oil. Add the finely chopped garlic with riced broccoli and sauté for 1 min. Season the rice with toasted sesame oil, coconut amino, and coarse salt. Fry for 2 min. more. The broccoli rice should be sautéed until it is just done and not mushy and maintains a bright green color.
2. Remove from heat and immediately add grated ginger to it. Also, add lime juice.
3. Sprinkle cilantro, sliced almonds and scallions. Arrange some lime wedges on the side and serve.

2. Low-carb vegan Grilled Tofu Skewers

Prep. Time: 15 minutes

Cook Time: 15 minutes

Servings: 6 servings

Serving size: 1 skewer

Nutrition as per serving

118kcal / 5.3g fat / 10g carbs / 1.8g fiber / 10.6g protein = 8g net carbs

Ingredients

- Tofu 1 block (180 g)
- Yellow bell pepper 1
- Zucchini 2 small
- Cherry tomatoes 2 cups
- Red bell pepper 1
- Red onion 1
- Soy sauce 2 tbsp.
- Barbecue sauce 3 tsp.
- Sesame seeds 2 tsp.
- Pepper
- Salt

Directions

1. Press the tofu to remove its liquid for at least half an hour. Afterward, cut it into cubes and soak in soy sauce
2. Cut the veggies: cut bell peppers, slice zucchini, and chop red onions into small squares. Every piece should be cut to the same size.
3. Prepare skewers: stick the veggies and tofu one after the other on bamboo sticks till all the vegetables have been used up.
4. Heat a grill pan or a frying pan till sizzling hot, brush some olive oil on it and assemble skewers in it, cooking for a few minutes on every side, till the veggies turn soft, not soggy, and the peppers begin getting a char. The tofu will turn golden brown. Sprinkle some pepper and salt when all is cooked, brush some barbecue sauce on the skewers, sprinkle on little sesame seeds. Take off from grill or pan.
5. Serve hot.

3. Zucchini Alfredo Pasta

Prep. Time: 15 minutes

Cook Time: 15 minutes

Servings: 2 Servings

Serving size: ½ of the recipe

Nutrition as per serving

225kcal / 16g fat / 19g carbs / 6g fiber / 14g protein = 12g net carbs

- **Ingredients**
- Zucchinis spiralized 2 medium
- Vegan Parmesan 1-2 Tbsp. (optional)
- Quick Alfredo Sauce
- Raw cashews soaked 1/2 cup
- Lemon juice 2 Tbsp.

- Garlic powder 1/2 tsp.
- Nutritional yeast 3 Tbsp.
- White miso (can sub soy sauce, coconut amino or tamari,) 2 tsp.
- Onion powder 1 tsp.
- Water ¼ - ½ cup

Directions

1. Spiralize the zucchini to make noodles. In a large saucepan, heat a little olive oil and add the zucchini noodles. Sauté for a few minutes and remove from heat.
2. Put all ingredients for the Alfredo into a blender (begin with ¼ cup water), then blend until creamy. If the sauce seems too thick, add a few tablespoons of water until the desired consistency is reached.
3. Top the zucchini noodles with hot Alfredo sauce and sprinkle a little vegan parmesan if desired.

4. Low-Carb Shiitake Mushroom Fried Rice

Prep. Time: 5 minutes

Cook Time: 25 minutes

Servings: 8 servings

Serving size: 1 cup

Nutrition as per serving

90kcal / 3g fat / 12g carbs / 5g fiber / 7g protein = 7g net carbs

Ingredients

- Frozen vegetables (peas, edamame, and carrots,) 10 oz.
- Frozen cauliflower rice 4 cups
- Frozen shiitake mushrooms 10 oz.
- Onion diced 1 medium
- Fresh ginger grated 2-inch
- Garlic minced 3 cloves
- Water 3-4 tbsp.
- Tamari, low-sodium 3 tbsp.
- Green onions, sliced thinly 1/2 cup
- Toasted sesame oil 1/2 tsp.

Directions

1. Over medium heat, fry the chopped onions with 3 to 4 tbsp. of water in a big pan until the onions are translucent and soft. Include the minced garlic and grated ginger. Combine all together and keep cooking until fragrant or for 2-3 minutes.

2. Add the cauliflower rice, mushrooms, and frozen mixed vegetables to the pan. Mix to combine, raising the flame to medium-high. Keep cooking for approx. 15 minutes or till all the veggies are tender and hot and also the water has evaporated.
3. A small bowl mix together toasted sesame oil and low-sodium tamari and pour on the veggies and mix it in. sprinkle sliced green onions and serve.

5. Portobello Pizza Keto Stuffed Mushrooms Recipe

Prep. Time: 10 minutes

Cook Time: 20 minutes

Servings: 4 servings

Serving size: 1 stuffed mushroom

Nutrition as per serving

113kcal / 6g fat / 5g carbs / 1g fiber / 7g protein = 4g net carbs

Ingredients

- Olive oil spray
- Portobello mushrooms, remove stems 4 large
- Marinara sauce, low-carb 1/2 cup
- Mozzarella cheese shredded 1/2 cup
- Pepperoni sausage (or a chorizo link, sliced thinly) 16 slices

Directions

1. Heat the oven up to 190 degrees C. Line parchment paper on a baking tray spraying it with olive oil spray.
2. Scoop out the dark gills of the mushrooms using a spoon, and throw away the gills.
3. Assemble the mushrooms with the stem side up, and on it, add 2 tbsp. of sauce on each. Add 2 tbsp. of mozzarella and four slices of pepperoni on each.
4. Put it in the oven for 20 to 25 minutes, till the cheese is melted and bubbly and the mushrooms are done. Serve hot.

6. Easy Broccoli Soup

Prep. Time: 10 minutes

Cook Time: 25 minutes

Servings: 6 servings

Serving size: 1 cup

Nutrition as per serving

171 kcal/ 13g fat / 8g carbs / 2g fiber / 3g protein = 6g net carbs

Ingredients

- Cauliflower florets 1 cup
- Broccoli 1 pound
- Vegan cheese cheddar style 1-2 tbsp. - optional
- Coconut milk full fat 1 cup
- Water 1 cup
- Onion 1 medium
- Bay leaves 2 small
- Garlic 2 cloves
- Olive oil 2 tbsp.
- Salt
- Nutritional yeasts 3 tbsp.
- Black pepper powder 1 tsp.

Directions

1. Over medium heat, add olive oil to a pan.
2. Add garlic and bay leaves and fry till the garlic is golden.
3. Add in the chopped onions and fry till they are translucent.

4. Add the cauliflower florets and fry for 2 minutes.
5. Put in the broccoli florets and fry for 8 minutes or till the raw odor is gone.
6. Take off heat. Leave it to cool, and then blend into a paste, adding a cup of water.
7. Put on the stove again, add the coconut milk and boil the mixture.
8. Then add the salt, black pepper, nutritional yeast, and keep on stirring.
9. Simmer for about 6-8 minutes. Serve hot!

7. Vegan Thai Soup

Prep. Time: 10 minutes

Cook Time: 15 minutes

Servings: 3-4 servings

Serving size: 1/4 of the recipe

Nutrition as per serving

339 kcal / 27.6g fat / 15.2g carbs / 3.2g fiber / 14.8g protein = 12g net carbs

Ingredients

- Mushrooms sliced 3
- Red onion, julienned 1/2
- Ginger root, peeled and chopped finely 1/2-inch piece
- Red bell pepper julienned 1/2
- Garlic, chopped finely 2 cloves
- Thai chili, chopped finely 1/2
- Water or preferably vegetable broth 2 cups
- Coconut sugar or any Keto substitute 1 tbsp.
- Coconut milk 1 can (14-oz.)
- Firm tofu, cut in squares 10 oz.
- Soy sauce or tamari 1 tbsp.
- Fresh cilantro, chopped a handful
- Lime juice 2 tsp.

Directions

1. In a big pot, add all the veggies (mushrooms, onion, garlic, ginger, red bell pepper, and Thai chili), coconut milk broth, and sugar.
2. Take it to a rolling boil and then let cook for 5 minutes over medium heat.
3. Then add the cubed tofu and cook for another 5 minutes.
4. Take off the heat, then add the lime juice, tamari, and fresh cilantro. Mix and serve.
5. Store the soup in an airtight container in the refrigerator for up to 6 days. It can also be frozen.

8. Cauliflower Fried Rice

Prep. Time: 5 minutes

Cook Time: 10 minutes

Servings: 2 servings

Serving size: 3 cups

Nutrition as per serving

289kcal / 14g fat / 30.2g carbs / 15g fiber / 12g protein = 15g net carbs

Ingredients

- Cauliflower, riced 1 small
- Garlic, minced 5 cloves
- Sesame oil 2 tbsp.
- Mixed vegetables (onions, peas, bell pepper, carrots,) 1 ½ cup
- Pepper to taste
- Salt, to taste

Optional add-ons:

- Thai peanut sauce
- Tamari 2 tbsp.
- Curry powder 2 tsp.
- Scallions, chopped 5
- Sesame seeds 4 tsp.

Directions

1. Wash and cut the cauliflower into florets. Put the florets into a food processor and process till it becomes rice-like.
2. In a large pot or pan, heat the sesame oil, and add minced garlic, carrots, onions, bell pepper, peas, and scallions if using. Sauté all for about 3 minutes.

3. Then add the cauliflower rice and sauté for another 5 minutes, add pepper and salt. Add the optional add-ons; Thai peanut sauce and curry powder, mix for 2 minutes. Take out in bowls or plates sprinkle with the sesame seeds if you like.

9. Indian Baingan Bharta

Prep. Time: 15 minutes

Cook Time: 15 minutes

Servings: 4 servings

Serving size: ¼ of the recipe

Nutrition as per serving

222kcal /14g fat / 23g carbs / 8g fiber / 4g protein = 15g net carbs

Ingredients

- Eggplants 2 medium
- Onion, sliced 1 medium
- Olive oil ¼ cup
- Garlic, diced 4 cloves
- Tomato chopped 1 medium
- Cumin seeds ½ tsp.
- Turmeric powder ½ tsp.
- Chili powder ½ tsp.
- Salt, to taste
- Green chili, chopped 1
- Fresh cilantro, chopped 1 sprig

Directions

1. On an open flame, roast both the eggplants. When one side is done, turn to cook the other side. The eggplant will shrink and sag, and the skins will become wrinkled when it is cooked from inside. Leave to cool, and then peel the skin as much as possible and mash.
2. In a frying pan or skillet, heat oil and sauté the onions till reddish brown. Add garlic and cumin.
3. Stir and add the tomatoes, chili powders, turmeric and salt. Fry on medium heat until the tomatoes become soft and all is cooked thoroughly.
4. Add the mashed eggplant to the tomato mixture and cook for a couple of minutes.
5. Sprinkle fresh cilantro and chopped green chili on top and serve.

Chapter 4- Salads

1. Vegan Arugula Avocado Tomato Salad

Prep. Time: 20 minutes

Servings: 8 servings

Serving size: 1cup

Nutrition as per serving

134kcal / 9g fat / 12g carbs / 10g fiber / 3g protein = 2g net carbs

Ingredients

For Balsamic Vinaigrette

- Lemon juice 1 tbsp.
- Balsamic vinegar 2 tbsp.
- Olive oil 1 tbsp.
- Maple syrup 1 tbsp.
- Black pepper 1/4 tsp.
- Garlic minced 1 small clove
- Himalayan pink salt 1/4 tsp.

For Arugula Salad

- Baby arugula chopped roughly 5 oz.
- Basil leaves sliced thinly 6 large
- Red and yellow grape tomatoes halve 1 pint each
- Avocados chopped 2 large

- Red onion minced 1/2 cup

Directions

1. In a large salad bowl, add the sliced basil leaves and roughly chopped arugula. Include the minced red onion, avocado chunks, and sliced grape tomatoes into the bowl. Mix to combine.
2. In a measuring cup, whisk together olive oil, balsamic vinegar, lemon juice, maple syrup, garlic clove, black pepper and salt, until combined well.
3. Drizzle all the balsamic dressing on the salad. Lightly mix the salad till all is coated in the dressing. Serve the salad on a large platter.

2. Triple Green Kale Salad

Prep. Time: 14 minutes

Cook Time: 1 minute

Servings: 4 servings

Serving size: ¼ of the recipe

Nutrition as per serving

135kcal / 10g fat / 10g carbs / 3g fiber / 3g protein = 7g net carbs

Ingredients

Green 1

- Lacinato kale, torn to small piece 8-10 oz.
- Toasted sesame oil 2 tsp.
- Flaxseed oil or olive oil extra virgin, 2 tsp.
- Garlic cloves, crushed or grated 2 small
- Fresh ginger grated 1 tsp.
- Coarse sea salt a pinch

Green 2

- Snow peas, cut into pieces, a large handful
- Coconut amino 2 tsp.
- Ripe avocado, sliced 1
- Balsamic vinegar 2 tsp.
- Scallions, cut into small pieces, a small handful
- Hemp seeds
- Orange zest

Directions

1. Wash and dry the kale thoroughly. On a cutting board, put the kale leaf and remove each leaf's center stems with a paring knife. Remove the stems from all the leaves. Pile 4-5 kale leaves and slice them into smaller pieces.

2. Mix the chopped kale leaves and all the ingredients of "green 1". Lightly massage the kale with clean hands, rubbing the oil with the leaves.
3. Add the ingredients of "green 2". Toss and serve chilled

3. Tomato Cucumber Salad

Prep. Time: 10 minutes

Servings: 4 servings

Serving size: 2 large portions or 4 small sides

Nutrition as per serving

176 kcal / 14g fat / 13g carbs / 5g fiber / 2g protein = 8g net carbs

Ingredients

- Green bell pepper 1
- Cherry tomatoes (quartered) 1 ½ cups
- Ripe avocados 1-2
- English cucumber 1
- Avocado oil 1/8 - 1/4 cup
- Red wine vinegar 1 tbsp.
- Lemon, juiced 1
- Fresh cilantro 2 tbsp.
- Pepper to taste
- Salt to taste

Directions

1. Cut the veggies, discarding any skin, seeds, and stems not needed.
2. Blend together oil, lemon juice, vinegar, pepper, salt, and fresh herbs that you like and drizzle all over the salad.
3. Mix together to coat well and serve!

4. Best Homemade Vegan Ranch

Prep. Time: 10 minutes

Servings: 8 servings

Serving size: 1½ tablespoon

Nutrition as per serving

138kcal / 11g fat / 8g carbs / 1g fiber / 5g protein = 7g net carbs

Ingredients

- Raw cashew pieces 1 1/2 cups
- Water 3/4 cup
- Rice vinegar 2 tbsp.
- Lemon juice 2 tbsp.
- Salt 1 tsp.
- Garlic powder 1 1/2 tsp.
- Onion powder 1 1/2 tsp.
- Fresh dill 1/4 cup of dried dill 2-3 tsp.

Directions

1. In hot water, soak the raw cashews for more than 5-10 minutes.
2. Strain the cashews and put them into a blender. Add all ingredients, excluding the dill, and process until very smooth.
3. Now include the dill, and give it a pulse or two to combine. Don't blend the dill; otherwise, it will be very green.
4. Drizzle on salads or as a dip with fresh veggies. Will keep in the fridge for up to 6 days. If it thickens in the fridge, add water to thin it out to the desired consistency

5. Vegan Sesame Ginger Coleslaw

Prep. Time: 30 minutes

Servings: 12 servings

Serving size: 1 cup

Nutrition as per serving

66kcal / 2g fat / 11g carbs / 3g fiber / 3g protein = 8g net carbs

Ingredients

For sesame ginger dressing -

- Almond butter 2 tbsp.
- Tahini 1 tbsp.
- Tamari, low-sodium 2 tbsp.

- Rice vinegar 2 tbsp.
- Fresh ginger peeled 2-inch knob
- Lime juice 3 tbsp.
- Hot sauce 1 tbsp.
- Garlic peeled 1 medium clove
- Maple syrup 1 tbsp.

For coleslaw -

- Red cabbage sliced thinly 5 cups
- Carrots sliced thinly 2 cups
- Green cabbage sliced thinly 5 cups
- Green onions sliced 1 cup
- Cilantro chopped roughly 1 cup

Directions

1. In a blender, add tahini. Almond butter, tamari, lime juice, rice vinegar, maple syrup, hot sauce, ginger and garlic clove, and blend on high speed until creamy and smooth.
2. In a large bowl, thinly sliced carrots, green and red cabbage, cilantro, and green onions. Drizzle the dressing all over the veggie mixture, and then toss to combine.
3. Refrigerate covered for 1 hour. Serve chilled

Notes

Before you add the dressing, salting the cabbage helps to draw out the extra liquid. This way, the slaw will not get soggy when stored for a few days in the fridge.

Chapter 5- Snacks

1. Vegan Lemon Curd

Prep. Time: 5 minutes

Cook Time: 10 minutes

Servings: 9 servings

Serving size: 1.75tbsp

Nutrition as per serving

5kcal / 0g fat / 0g carbs / 0g fiber / 0g protein = 0g net carbs

Ingredients

- Lemon 1 large
- Almond milk or coconut milk 1 cup
- Lemon stevia or monk fruit drops ¼ tsp.
- Xanthum gum 1 tsp.
- Turmeric powder a pinch optional

Directions

1. In a blender, blend together almond milk, lemon juice and zest from a large lemon and stevia lemon/monk fruit drops
2. Transfer the mixture to a medium saucepan. Slowly stir in xanthum gum. Boil the mixture and remove it from heat.
3. Transfer to a container. Leave it to cool before covering. It will thicken as it gets cold. Keep in the refrigerator for up to a week.

2. Crispy Cauliflower Wings

Prep. Time: 5 minutes

Cook Time: 40 minutes

Servings: 6 servings

Serving size: 1 cup

Nutrition as per serving

48kcal / 4.3g fat / 1g carbs / 1g fiber / 2g protein = 0g net carbs

Ingredients

- Hot sauce 3-4 tbsp.
- Almond flour 1 tbsp.
- Avocado oil 1 tbsp.
- Salt to taste
- Cauliflower head (cut into bites, washed and pat dried) 1

Directions

1. Heat oven up to 180c / 160c / 350f /gas 6.
2. Combine avocado oil, almond flour, hot sauce and salt together in a large mixing bowl.
3. Mix in the cauliflower and coat well.
4. In a single layer, assemble the cauliflower on a foil-lined baking sheet.
5. Bake for 35-40 min. Halfway through, take out the baking sheet, mix the cauliflower, and bake until its edges are crispy and done. Take out and put aside.
6. Serve warm or cold according to your preference, with some hot sauce dip

3. Vegan Seed Cheese

Prep. Time: 10 minutes

Servings: 6

Serving size: 1 tablespoon

Nutrition as per serving

150kcal / 11g fat / 3g carbs / 3g fiber / 7g protein = 0g net carbs

Ingredients

- Seeds sunflower, pumpkin, or a blend 1 cup
- Water 1/2 cup
- Apple cider vinegar 2 tbsp.
- Nutritional yeast 2 tbsp.
- Salt ¼ tsp. suppose using salted seeds/ if using unsalted seeds ¾ tsp.
- Seasonings to taste

Directions

1. Combine all ingredients in a food processor and process.
2. Leave for ten minutes.
3. Process again until creamy and smooth.
4. Enjoy!

4. Easy & Authentic Guacamole

Prep. Time: 10 minutes

Servings: 4 servings

Serving size: ½ cup

Nutrition as per serving

184.8kcal / 15.3g fat / 12.3g carbs / 7.6g fiber / 2.5g protein = 5g net carbs

Ingredients

- Avocados, ripe 3
- Onion, diced finely 1/2 small
- Roma tomatoes, diced 2
- Fresh cilantro finely chopped 3 tbsp.
- Jalapeno pepper, finely diced and seeds removed 1
- Garlic, minced2 cloves
- Lime juice 1
- Sea salt 1/2 tsp.

Directions

1. Cut the avocados into halves, removing the pit; scoop the avocado pulp into a large mixing bowl.
2. With a fork, mash the avocado pulp making it as smooth or chunky as you would like.
3. Add all the other ingredients and mix. Taste and modify seasoning by adding more lime juice or a pinch of salt if needed.
4. Pour the guacamole into a serving bowl and serve with low-carb Keto crackers (recipe below).

5. Almond Flour Low-Carb Keto Crackers

Prep. Time: 10 minutes

Cook Time: 15 minutes

Servings: 6 Servings

Serving size: ½ cup

Nutrition as per serving

151kcal / 13g fat / 6g carbs / 3g fiber / 4g protein = 3g net carbs

Ingredients

- Almond flour 1 cup
- Sunflower seeds 2 tbsp.
- Flax meal or whole psyllium husks 1 tablespoon
- Sea salt ¾ tsp. Or to taste
- Water 2 tbsp.
- Olive oil or coconut oil one tablespoon

Directions

1. Heat oven up to 350°f.
2. In a food processor, blend together sunflower seeds, almond flour, sea salt and psyllium, until the sunflower seeds are finely chopped.
3. Add in the coconut and oil-water and pulse until a dough forms
4. Place a parchment paper on a flat surface and place and press the dough ball flat on it. Top with another parchment sheet and roll the dough to a thickness of ⅛ - 1/16 of an inch.
5. Remove the top parchment sheet, and with a knife or pizza cutter, cut into one-inch squares. If desired, sprinkle with sea salt.
6. Transfer the cut dough onto a baking tray and bake in a preheated oven at 350°f until edges are crisp and brown (around 10-15 minutes). Leave on a rack to cool and breaks into squares.

6. Oven-Baked Healthy Zucchini Chips

Prep. Time: 10 minutes

Cook Time: 2 hours

Servings: 8 servings

Serving size: 12 zucchini chips

Nutrition as per serving

23kcal / 2g fat / 2g carbs / 1g fiber / 1g protein = 1g net carbs

Ingredients

- Zucchini 2 medium
- Avocado oil (or olive oil) 1 tbsp.
- Sea salt 1/2 tsp

Directions

1. Heat the oven up to 93 degrees C (200 degrees F).
2. Slice the zucchini into .3 cm (1/8 in) thin slices.

3. Toss the zucchini slices in olive oil and coat them thoroughly. Lightly sprinkle with salt. Mix to coat again.

4. Place a cooling rack covered with parchment paper on two cookie trays. (This method permits better circulation of air.) In a single layer, assemble the zucchini slices on it. Do not overlap.

5. Put in the oven for about two and a half hours, turning the pans 90 degrees halfway through. When the zucchini chips begin to get golden and crispy, they are. Turn off the oven and leave them there to cool with the door open slightly (as they cool, they will become crisper).

7. 8-Ingredient Zucchini Lasagna

Prep. Time: 20 minutes

Cook Time: 1 hour

Servings: 9 squares

Serving size: 1 square

Nutrition as per serving

395kcal / 35.3g fat / 19g carbs / 10g fiber / 6.8g protein = 9g net carbs

Ingredients

- Organic tomato basil marinara sauce 1 jars (28-oz.)
- Zucchini squash, sliced thinly 3 medium (or substitute with eggplant)

For vegan ricotta

- Soaked blanched almonds or raw macadamia nuts 3 cups (or extra firm tofu, strained and dry pressed for 10 minutes 1 block of 16-oz.)
- Nutritional yeast 2 tbsp.
- Fresh basil chopped finely 1/2 cup
- Dried oregano 2 tsp.
- Lemon, medium 2 Tbsp.
- Olive oil, extra virgin 1 tbsp. (optional)
- Sea salt 1 tsp.
- Black pepper a pinch
- Water 1/2 cup
- Vegan parmesan cheese 1/4 cup + more for topping (optional)

Directions

1. Heat oven up to 375 degrees F
2. Add almond or macadamia nuts or crumbled tofu to a blender or food processor and combine and scrape down the sides when needed. It should become a fine meal.
3. Then include the remaining ingredients: fresh basil, Nutritional yeast, oregano, olive oil (if using), lemon juice, pepper, salt, vegan parmesan cheese (if using) and water. It should become a well-puréed paste or mixture.

4. Check the seasonings, and add more pepper and salt for flavor, lemon juice for vividness and nutritional yeast for cheesier flavor, as needed.

5. Pour about a cup of marinara sauce into a baking dish of 9×13-inch and assemble the thinly sliced zucchini in overlapping lines.

6. Place small scoops of the vegan ricotta mixture all over the layered zucchini and spread it gently into a thin layer. Apply a layer of the marinara sauce and then layer more zucchini slices. Carry on till all zucchini and filling are used up. The zucchini and sauce should be the last two layers. Scatter some vegan parmesan cheese (if using) on top, covering with the foil.

7. Place in oven covered to bake for 45 minutes, then take off the foil and bake for another 15 minutes. When done, the zucchini should tender enough to be easily pierced with a knife. Leave to rest for 10 to 15 minutes.

8. Serve hot with fresh basil and more vegan parmesan cheese on top. Keep Leftovers in the refrigerator for 2-3 days, or freeze for up to 1 month.

8. Sunflower Courgetti Seed Cheese

Prep. Time: 20 minutes

Servings: 6 servings

Serving size: 2 tablespoon

Nutrition as per serving

286cals / 22g fat / 17gcarbs / 8g fiber / 13g protein = 4g net carbs

Ingredients

- Sunflower seeds 1 cup
- Zucchini /courgette 3
- Nutritional yeast 3 tbsp.
- Garlic 1 clove
- Sesame seeds 3 tbsp.
- Turmeric ¼ tsp.
- Apple cider vinegar 1 tbsp.
- Salt 2 pinches
- Water for blending and soaking
- Cherry tomatoes 6
- Fresh basil leaves 12

Directions

1. Immerse the sunflower seeds in water with a pinch of salt overnight or for at least an hour.

2. Strain the sunflower seeds and place them in a blender with garlic, nutritional yeast, turmeric, sesame, and vinegar.

3. Just add enough water into the blender so that it turns into a smooth paste.

4. A spiralizer makes the zucchini /courgette into noodles or makes them into thin strips with a vegetable peeler.

5. Add a pinch of salt to the spiralized noodles and massage them until it reduces in volume and releases its juices.
6. Mix in the cheese mixture and enjoy.

9. Vegan Garlic Aioli

Prep. Time: 5 minutes

Servings: 8 servings

Serving size: 1 tablespoon

Nutrition as per serving

138kcal / 14g fat / 2g carbs / 1g fiber / 1g protein = 1g net carbs

Ingredients

- Original vegenaise 3/4 cup
- Fresh lemon juice 2 ½ tbsp.
- Garlic minced 3 medium cloves
- Himalayan pink salt ¼ tsp.
- Black pepper¼ tsp

Directions

In a small bowl, add all the ingredients and combine with a whisk. Refrigerate covered for 30 minutes. Serve chilled.

Notes

Store the remaining aioli in a sealed container in the refrigerator for 5 to 7 days.

Vegan garlic aioli cannot be frozen as vegan mayo splits, and the consistency doesn't remain the same.

Chapter 6- Side Dishes

1. Asian Cucumber Salad

Prep. Time: 10 minutes

Wait Time: 15 minutes

Servings: 2

Serving size: 1.5 cups

Nutrition as per serving

70 cal. / 14.3g fat / 6g carbs / 3g fiber / 3g protein = 3g net carbs

Ingredients

- Scallions, thinly sliced 2
- English cucumber 1
- Table salt 1/4 tsp.
- For the dressing:
- Soy sauce 2 tsp.
- Toasted sesame oil 2 tsp.
- Rice vinegar or white vinegar 1 tsp.
- Sesame seeds, white or black 1/2 tsp.
- Red pepper flakes crushed 1/2 tsp.

Directions

1. Prepping the cucumber: slice 1/2-inch thick rounds of the cucumber, then chop each coin into 3 to 5 small wedges. In a medium bowl, sprinkle salt on the wedges and toss. Leave it at room temperature until they release liquid, about 15 to 30 minutes. Discard the liquid and pat dry the cucumber wedges with a paper towel to absorb moisture until the wedges are almost dry to touch.
2. Mix the salad: To a bowl, add the dried cucumbers, scallions and all ingredients for the dressing. Stir until combined. After tasting, add more dressing ingredients if required.
3. Serving: serve immediately after preparation; otherwise, the cucumbers will release more water and lose their crunch. Serve it as a side dish or refreshing appetizer with heavy meat-centric meals like chicken adobo, beef stir fry, or pork stir fry.

2. Oven Roasted Lemon Garlic Asparagus

Prep. Time: 10 minutes

Cook Time: 12 minutes

Servings: 4

Serving size: ¼ of the recipe

Nutrition as per serving

67kcal / 4g fat / 5 g carbs / 2g fiber / 2g protein = 3g net carbs

Ingredients

- Asparagus (1/2 inch thick stalks about 25-30) 1 lb.
- Olive oil 1 tbsp.
- Dried thyme 1/4 tsp.
- Vegan parmesan cheese 1-2 tbsp.
- Onion granules 1/4 tsp.
- Garlic, minced 2 cloves
- Lemon zest 1 tsp.
- Himalayan sea salt to taste
- Pepper to taste
- Fresh lemon juice 1 tbsp.
- Lemon 4-5 slices
- Olive oil 1 tsp.

Directions

1. Heat the oven up to 425 degrees.
2. Prepare the Asparagus: Wash and dry the asparagus thoroughly. Cut the base of each stalk of 1 to 1 ½ inch off the bottom.
3. Line a tray with parchment and place the asparagus spears on it. Drizzle a tablespoon of olive oil all over the asparagus spears and mix to coat each piece. Add onion granules,

thyme, lemon zest, pepper and sea salt all over the oiled asparagus and mix one more time. Place lemon slices on top and bake for about 8 minutes.

4. In a small bowl, add the crushed garlic cloves and a tablespoon of olive oil and mix both together. When the asparagus has baked for 8 minutes, remove the tray, add the minced garlic evenly all over the asparagus. Place it back in the oven and again bake for 3 to 4 more minutes.

5. Take out the tray when the asparagus is tender; it must still be bright green and not mushy. Squeeze about a tablespoon of lemon over the asparagus and sprinkle with shredded vegan parmesan cheese.

3. Zucchini Noodles with Avocado Sauce

Prep. Time: 10 minutes

Servings: 2

Serving size: 1/2 of the recipe

Nutrition as per serving

313kcal / 26.8g fat / 18.7g carbs / 9.7g fiber / 6.8g protein = 9 g net carbs

Ingredients

- Zucchini 1
- Cherry tomatoes sliced 12
- Basil 1 1/4 cup
- Avocado 1
- Pine nuts 4 tbsp.
- Water 1/3 cup
- Lemon juice 2 tbsp.

Directions

1. Using a spiralizer or a peeler, cut the zucchini noodles.
2. Apart from the cherry tomatoes, put all the ingredients in a blender and blend until smooth to make avocado sauce.
3. Combine avocado sauce, zucchini noodles, and cherry tomatoes in a large mixing bowl.
4. It's recommended to serve these avocado sauce zucchini noodles fresh, but they can also be stored in the fridge for about 1 to 2 days.

4. Zucchini Tomato Pesto Veggie Bake

Prep. Time: 25 minutes

Cook Time: 35 minutes

Servings: 6

Serving size: 1/6 of the recipe

Nutrition as per serving

127kcal / 9g fat / 11g carbs / 3g fiber / 3g protein = 8g net carbs

Ingredients

Pesto sauce

- Fresh basil leaves 2 cups
- Garlic peeled 1 clove
- Pine nuts 1/4 cup (or raw pumpkin seeds)
- Olive oil 3 tbsp.
- Lemon juice 2 tbsp.
- Black pepper 1/8 tsp.
- Himalayan pink salt 1/4 tsp.

Vegetables

- Zucchini sliced thinly 3 medium
- Red onions sliced thinly 4 small
- Roma tomatoes sliced thinly 8 medium
- Olive oil 1 tbsp.

Directions

1. Prepare the pesto sauce. Add the fresh pumpkin seeds, basil leaves, garlic, olive oil, lemon juice, water pepper, salt, and a food processor or blender. Blend the sauce till smooth and put it aside for the future.
2. Heat the oven to 350 degrees. Slice thinly the red onions, zucchini, and tomatoes, about 1/8"-1/4" thick. Make sure the veggies are cut in uniform size to bake evenly.

3. Lightly oil a cast-iron skillet with a brush. Assemble the sliced veggies in the skillet in the following order: zucchini, red onion, zucchini, and tomato. Keep on the process till all the veggies are done with. Begin in the outer edge first, going in circles towards the center.
4. Pour the vegan pesto sauce evenly all over the veggies, and then with a silicone brush, spread the sauce all over the veggies in the pan.
5. Top a sheet of unbleached parchment paper on the veggies and put in the oven for 30-35 minutes or till all the veggies are tender.

5. Tomato Mushroom Spaghetti Squash

Prep. Time: 30 minutes

Cook Time: 10 minutes

Servings: 6

Serving size: 1 bowl

Nutrition as per serving

173 kcal/ 12g fat / 17g carbs / 4g fiber / 4g protein = 12g net carbs

Ingredients

* Spaghetti squash, 1 large, about 6 cups.
* Tomatoes diced 2 cups
* Garlic minced 4 cloves
* Mushrooms sliced 8 oz.
* Onions or shallots, chopped, 1/3 cup about 1 small
* Pine nuts toasted 1/4 cup
* Fresh basil, a handful,
* Olive oil 3 tbsp.
* Black pepper to taste
* Kosher salt to taste
* red pepper flakes pinch

Directions

1. Cook the spaghetti squash. Once sufficiently cool, slice in half, discard seeds and stringy pieces and strip with 2 forks. Put it aside.
2. Heat oil in a large frypan over medium heat. Fry mushrooms and onions, stirring continuously, for about 3 to 4 minutes. Add in garlic and stir until fragrant, 1 to 2 minutes. Don't overcook the garlic.
3. Include tomatoes and keep stirring.
4. Include the cooked spaghetti squash, then toss till squash is heated through and veggies are evenly distributed.
5. Stir in toasted pine nuts and fresh basil. Season with pepper, a pinch of red pepper flakes and kosher salt to taste

6. Roasted Cabbage with Lemon

Prep. Time: 5 minutes

Cook Time: 30 minutes

Servings: 4

Serving size: 1

Nutrition as per serving

78 kcal / 7g fat / 5g carbs / 1g fiber / 1g protein = 4g net carbs

Ingredients

- Green cabbage 1 large head
- Olive oil 2 tbsp.
- Freshly squeezed lemon juice 3 tbsp.
- sea salt a generous amount
- black pepper freshly ground a generous amount
- lemon slices, (optional)

Directions

1. Heat the oven up to 450f. Apply non-stick spray on a roasting pan.
2. Cutting through the stem end and core, slice the cabbage's head into eight same-size wedges. Place wedges in the roasting pan in a single layer.
3. Mix the lemon juice and olive oil. With a pastry brush, apply the mixture on each cabbage wedge, then generously season with fresh ground black pepper salt. Flip over the cabbage wedges carefully, and brush and season this side too.
4. Bake the cabbage until the wedges' undersides are nicely browned, for about 15 minutes. Removing the pan from the oven, flip each wedge carefully.
5. Place in the oven again and roast for 10 to 15 minutes more, till the wedges are cooked thoroughly, nicely brown and with a bit of chewiness remaining.
6. Serve immediately, with extra lemon slices.

7. Keto Roasted Radishes

Prep. Time: 5 minutes

Cook Time: 30 minutes

Servings: 6

Serving size: 1 cup

Nutrition as per serving

25kcal / 1g fat / 1g carbs / 1g fiber / 1g protein = 0g net carbs

Ingredients

- Radishes 20-25 (similar size)
- Vegetable broth 1/2 cup
- Garlic minced 3 cloves
- Dried rosemary 1/2 tsp.
- Fresh rosemary 1 sprig (optional)
- Dried oregano 1/4 tsp.
- Onion Powder 1/2 tsp.
- Black pepper 1/4 tsp.
- Salt 1/4 tsp.

Directions

1. Heat the oven up to 400 degrees.
2. Prep the radishes by rinsing them well and cutting off the roots greens, and stems. Chop each radish in half. Make into quarters if they are bigger to cook quickly.
3. In a medium-sized casserole, add the minced garlic, vegetable broth, onion powder, rosemary, oregano, black pepper and salt. Stirring well to mix the seasonings.
4. Transfer all the radishes into the casserole, toss with the broth to coat all radishes and then bake, covered for about 30-35 minutes (if the radishes are on the small side, check them at 25 minutes) or till the radishes are tender, stirring in between.
5. Sprinkle fresh rosemary just before serving (optional). Keep leftovers in a sealed container in the refrigerator for 4-5 days.

Chapter 7- Desserts

1. Easy Vegan Fat Bombs

Prep. Time: 10 minutes

Freeze Time: 1-2 hours

Servings: 12 fat bombs

Serving size: 3 fat bombs

Nutrition as per serving

320 kcal / 35g fat / 5g carbs / 3g fiber / 3g protein = 2g net carbs

Ingredients

- Stevia 6 drops
- Macadamia nut butter warmed ¾ cup
- Coconut oil, melted or room temperature ¼ cup

Directions

1. In the microwave or a saucepan, heat macadamia nut butter until warm.
2. Pour in coconut oil and stevia drops. Mix.
3. Spoon mixture into mini muffin tins or silicone molds and chill for about 1-2 hours.
4. When set, take out of molds and enjoy!
5. Keep in a sealed box in the freezer.

2. Coconut Fat Bombs

Prep. Time: 10 minutes

Freeze Time: 1 hour

Servings: 18

Serving size: 1 fat bomb

Nutrition as per serving

86kcal / 9g fat / 1g carbs / 0g fiber / 0g protein = 1g net carbs

Ingredients

- Coconut Butter melted ½ cup
- Coconut finely shredded 2 tbsp. + ¼ cup
- Coconut oil, melted ½ cup
- Stevia 12 drops

Directions

1. Combine all ingredients; fill an ice cube tray or mini muffin liners with a tablespoon putting one spoonful in each. Chill for 1 hour. Keep in the fridge.

3. Peanut butter coconut truffles

Prep. Time: 20 minutes

Freeze Time: 1 hour 10 minutes

Servings: 22 truffles

Serving size: 2 truffles

Nutrition as per serving

126kcal / 11g fat / 4g carbs / 1g fiber / 3g protein = 3g net carbs

Ingredients

- Creamy peanut butter ½ cup
- Coconut oil 1 tbsp.
- Toasted coconut butter, melted ½ cup
- Shredded coconut, ½ cup + more to garnish
- Chopped peanuts, ½ cup + more to garnish
- Sea salt, ¼ tsp. optional
- Sugar-free chocolate ⅔ cup
- Stevia 10 drops

Directions

2. In a large mixing bowl, mix together the melted coconut butter, peanut butter, chopped peanuts, coconut, stevia drops and salt. Tasting to adjust amounts of salt and stevia if desired.

3. Chill until firm, for 1 hour.

4. Use a tablespoon and scoop out balls from the chilled PB mixture onto the baking sheet or a plate. Shape into a ball using your hands and do the same with all of the PB mixtures. Chill in the freezer or refrigerator and melt the chocolate.

5. Place the coconut oil and chocolate in a liquid measuring cup or a microwave-proof bowl in a microwave. Heat up for 1 minute, take out and mix. If it is not entirely melted, again microwave for 15-second intervals, stirring between each until completely smooth.

6. With a fork, roll each coconut peanut butter ball in the chocolate and drip off any excess chocolate. Then place on a baking sheet or plate -lined with parchment. Sprinkle chopped peanuts or toasted coconut on the balls, if desired.

7. Chill until chocolate is hard, for about 10 minutes. Keeps in the refrigerator for about a month.

4. Chocolate Coconut Almond Fat Bombs

Prep. Time: 10 minutes

Servings: 30 fat bombs

Serving size: 2 fat bombs

Nutrition as per serving

72kcal / 7g fat / 1g carbs / 1g fiber / 0g protein = 0g net carbs

Ingredients

- Cacao powder ¼ cup
- Cacao nibs ¼ cup
- Coconut oil, melted ½ cup
- Coconut Butter melted ½ cup
- Almonds crushed or sliced ¼ cup
- Stevia 10 drops (or erythritol ½ tsp.)
- Almond extracts 1 tsp.
- Vanilla extracts ½ tsp.
- Coconut, unsweetened & finely shredded ¼ cup

Directions

1. Mix coconut butter, coconut oil, cacao powder, vanilla extract, almond extract, erythritol, or stevia. If adding erythritol: heat on the stove or in the microwave for 1 to 2 minutes, it is dissolved. There should be no crunchy erythritol crystals.

2. Mix in the slivered or crushed almonds, cacao nibs and coconut flakes. With the tablespoon's help, fill an ice cube tray or mini cupcake liners, putting one spoonful in each. Keep in the fridge.

5. Mexican Spiced Keto Chocolate

Prep. Time: 10 minute

Servings: 18 pieces

Serving size: 1 piece

Nutrition as per serving

40kcal / 3g fat / 6g carbs / 1g fiber / 3g protein = 5g net carbs

Ingredients

- Cocoa powder 1/2 cup
- Cacao butter melted 1/4 cup
- Nutmeg 1/8 tsp.
- Cinnamon 1/4 tsp.
- Chili powder 1/2 tsp.
- Stevia, 25 drops
- Fine sea salt 1 pinch
- Black pepper 1 pinch
- Vanilla extracts 1/4 tsp.

Directions

1. In a medium mixing bowl, mix the dry ingredients together. Put aside.
2. Melt the cacao butter into a microwave-proof bowl on high for 30-second intervals until melted. Stir in between.
3. To the melted butter, add the stevia and vanilla.
4. Pour this cacao butter mixture into the dry mixture and mix until smooth.
5. Split the mixture between slightly greased baking trays or two loaf pans.
6. Leave it to solidify at room temperature. When set, break into 18 pieces.
7. Keep in a sealed box at room temperature for about 5 days.

6. Chocolate Almond Avocado Pudding Recipe

Prep. Time: 5 minutes

Servings: 3

Serving size: 1 cup

Nutrition as per serving

288 kcal / 14.3g fat / 12g carbs / 8g fiber / 5g protein = 4g net carbs

Ingredients

- Almond milk 1 1/2 cups
- Erythritol blends /granulated stevia 3 tbsp.
- Coconut cream 1/2 cup
- Avocado peeled & pitted medium 1 (6 oz.)
- Almond extracts 1 tsp.
- Cocoa powder unsweetened 3 tbsp.
- Vanilla extracts 1 tsp.
- Almonds sliced for garnish (optional)
- Coconut flakes, unsweetened for garnish (optional)

Directions

1. Blend all the ingredients in a power blender until smooth.
2. Pour into 3 cups, cover and chill for at least 5 hours or, if possible, overnight before serving.
3. Sprinkle sliced almonds and unsweetened coconut flakes before serving.

Chapter 8- 7 Day Sample Meal Plan:

While the keto vegan diet can sound rather restricting, many meals can indeed be produced with vegan-friendly items. Here is a 7-day meal plan with the recipes provided in this cookbook to kick start your keto vegan journey to shed weight.

Monday

- Breakfast: low-carb keto oatmeal
- Lunch: mashed cauliflower with garlic and herbs
- Dinner: easy broccoli soup with vegan arugula avocado salad

Tuesday

- Breakfast: vegan scrambled eggs.
- Lunch: Thai Zucchini noodles with Asian cucumber salad.
- Dinner: cauliflower fried rice with vegan cheese.

Wednesday

- Breakfast: overnight vegan keto Chia pudding
- Lunch: Vegan Thai soup.
- Dinner: Keto mac and cheese with Keto cheese sauce.

Thursday

- Breakfast: tofu shakshuka
- Lunch: lo-carb vegan tahini bowl
- Dinner. Portobello pizza keto stuffed mushrooms.

Friday

- Breakfast: vegan bulletproof coffee and avocado.
- Lunch: creamy tomato soup with oven-roasted lemon garlic asparagus.
- Dinner: Indian baingan bharta with oven-baked healthy zucchini chips.

Saturday

- Breakfast: Vegan keto smoothie with full-fat coconut milk, almond butter, cocoa powder and vegan protein powder.
- Lunch: Low-Carb Shiitake Mushroom Fried Rice.
- Dinner: Cauliflower fried rice with Sunflower Courgetti Seed Cheese.

Sunday

- Breakfast: Vegan keto protein smoothie bowl.
- Lunch: red curry cauliflower soup with Triple green kale salad.
- Dinner: zucchini Alfredo pasta with guacamole and crackers.

Vegan keto snacks

Try these vegan-friendly snacks to hold the hunger in the balance between meals:

- Nuts and coconut bars
- Sliced cucumber and vegan cream cheese spread
- Roasted peanuts or pumpkin seeds
- Guacamole with sliced bell pepper
- Coconut fat bombs (high-fat snacks/dessert made with shredded coconut oil and coconut butter)
- Trail mix with unsweetened coconut mixed nuts, and seeds
- Cocoa smoothie and coconut milk
- Dried unsweetened coconut flakes
- Olives stuffed with vegan cheese
- Celery sticks with almond butter dip
- Cauliflower tater tots
- Coconut cream with berries
- Coconut milk yogurt garnished with chopped almonds

There are so many delicious items to select from when on a vegan keto diet. Snacks and meals should be low in carbs and high in healthy fats.

Conclusion

Having a healthy, illness-free body is the goal for everybody. Physical exercise, a strict nutritious diet and a healthy lifestyle are the best ways to promote good health.

Vegan and Ketogenic diets are two of today's main wellness trends. While these two may not seem like they match together with each other because the vegan diet focuses mostly on a high quantity of carbs as the main source of nourishment, and the Keto diet limits carbs to 20-25g per day. Hence, vegans may still adopt a Ketogenic regimen, enabling them to attain the beneficial effects of each.

The Keto vegan diet is a high-fat, moderate protein, low-carb diet that eliminates all meat and dairy products. Vegetable-based Ketogenic diet ingredients contain vegetables lowest in carbs, almonds and all kinds of nuts and seeds, vegan protein sources, beans, coconut and healthy oils.

Vegans who follow a Vegan Ketogenic diet should consume unprocessed and natural foods in addition to low-carb vegan foods and avoid vegan foods that are highly processed.

High-carb foods like sweetened drinks, grains, and starchy vegetables (like potatoes, peas, turnips), should be eliminated when adopting a vegan-based Ketogenic diet.

Certain minerals and vitamins, including iron and vitamins B12 and vitamin D, should be taken to ensure that nutritional specifications are fulfilled.

High-fat and low-carb diets should not be used during pregnancy, breastfeeding, infancy, or while recovering from such medical conditions. If you are unsure about the Vegan Keto diet is the correct option for you, obtain support and guidance from your physician.

The Healthy Keto Meal Prep Cookbook with Pictures

Bend the Rules to Lose Weight Tasting Tens of Easy-to-Prep Ketogenic Recipes On a Budget

By

Jamie Carter

Table of Contents

Introduction

Few aspects are as well known in nutrition research as the tremendous health advantages of low-carb and ketogenic diets. Not only can these diets increase the cholesterol, blood pressure and blood sugar, but they also reduce your appetite, promote weight control and decrease the triglycerides.

A ketogenic diet may be an interesting way to manage such disorders and could accelerate weight loss. Yet it is challenging to follow, because it may be high on red meat and other oily, dried, and salty foods that are notoriously unhealthy. We still may not know anything about the long-term consequences, presumably because it's too hard to stay with that people can't eat this way for a long time. It is also important to note that "yo-yo diets" that contribute to rapid weight loss fluctuation are correlated with increased mortality. Instead of joining in the next common diet that will last just a few weeks or months (for most people that requires a ketogenic diet), strive to accept progress that is manageable over the long term. A healthy, unprocessed diet, abundant in very colorful fruits and vegetables, lean meats, seafood, whole grains, almonds, peas, olive oil, and plenty of water seems to provide the strongest evidence for a long, healthier, vibrant existence.

If you're interested to improve your fitness, this diet book might be worth considering.

Chapter 1: Keto Diet

The ketogenic (keto) diet is commonly known for having a diet (low crab), where the body creates ketones in the liver to be used as energy. It's alluded to by several different names – ketogenic diet, low carb diet, low carb high fat (LCHF), etc. When you consume something rich in carbohydrates, the body can release glucose and insulin.

Glucose is the simplest molecule for the body to transform and use as energy such that it can be preferred over some other energy source.

Insulin is created to process the glucose in your bloodstream by taking it across the body.

The glucose is being used as primary energy; the fats are not required and are thus processed. Usually, on a regular, higher carbohydrate diet, the body can use glucose as the key energy source. By lowering the consumption of carbohydrates, the body is induced into a condition known as ketosis. Ketosis, a normal mechanism the body initiates to help us live while food consumption is limited. During this state, we create ketones, which are formed by the oxidation of fats in the liver.

The ultimate aim of a well-controlled keto diet is to push your body into this physiological condition. We don't do this by deprivation of calories or starvation of carbohydrates.

What Do I Eat on a Keto Diet?

To initiate a keto diet, you may want to prepare accordingly. That implies getting a viable diet plan ready a. What you consume depends on how quickly you choose to get into a ketogenic condition, i.e., ketosis. The further stringent you are on your carbohydrates (less than 25g net carbs a day), the sooner you can reach ketosis.

You want to keep your carbs limited, come more from fruits, nuts, and dairy. Don't consume some processed grains such as wheat (bread, pasta, and cereals), starch (potatoes, beans, legumes) or berries. The small exceptions to this are banana, star fruit, and berries which may be eaten in moderation.

Do Not Eat

Grains: grain, maize, cereal, rice, etc.

Sugar: honey, maple syrup, agave, etc.

Fruit: bananas, grapes, strawberries, etc.

Tubers: yams, potatoes, etc.

Do Eat

Meats: fish, meat, lamb, chickens, chickens, etc.

Leafy Greens: lettuce, cabbage, etc.

Vegetables: broccoli, cauliflower, etc.

Low Fat Dairy: strong cheeses, high-fat milk, butter, etc.

Nuts and seeds: macadamias, walnuts, sunflower seeds, etc.

Avocado and berries – raspberries, blackberries, and other low glycemic

Sweeteners: stevia, erythritol, monk berries, and other low-carb sweeteners

Other fats: palm oil, high-fat salad dressing, fatty fats, etc.

Benefits of a Ketogenic Diet

Several advantages come from being on keto: from weight reduction and improved energy levels to medicinal uses. Mostly, everyone can easily profit from consuming a low-carb, high-fat diet. Below, you'll find a concise list of the advantages you may get from a ketogenic diet.

Weight Loss

The ketogenic diet actually utilizes your body fat as an energy source – but there are clear weight-loss advantages. On keto, your insulin (the fat-storing hormone) level drops greatly and transforms your body into a fat-burning process. Scientifically, the ketogenic diet has demonstrated better outcomes relative to low-fat and high-carb diets, also in the long run.

Control Blood Sugar

Keto reduces blood sugar levels due to the kinds of diet you consume. Studies also suggest that the ketogenic diet is a more efficient way to treat and avoid diabetes relative to low-calorie diets.

If you're pre-diabetic or have Type II diabetes, you should strongly try a ketogenic diet. We have several readers who have had experience in their blood sugar management on keto.

Mental Focus

Many people use the ketogenic diet primarily for improved mental output. Ketones are a perfect source of food for the brain. When you reduce carb consumption, you stop major increases in blood sugar. Together, which will help in increased attention and concentration? Studies suggest that an improved consumption of fatty acids may have affecting benefits to our brain's function.

Increased Energy & Normalized Hunger

By providing your body a stronger and more stable energy supply, you can feel more energized throughout the day. Fats are the most powerful molecule to burn as heat. On top of that, fat is inherently more rewarding and ends up keeping us in a satiated ("full") condition for longer.

Types of Ketogenic Diets

Many people wonder whether carbs are required to grow muscle. Actually, they're not. If you're asking this question, I will presume you know how you accumulate mass.

Your glycogen reserves will also be refilled while on a ketogenic diet. A keto diet is an effective way to grow muscle, but protein consumption is essential here. It's proposed that if you are trying to grow muscle, you could be getting in between 1.0 – 1.2g protein per lean pound of body mass. Putting muscle on can be slower on a ketogenic diet, but that's because the overall body fat is not growing as much.

If, for any reason, you need to add on body fat, too, you will accomplish your targets by various forms of a Ketogenic Diet. There are:

Standard Ketogenic Diet (SKD): This is the classic keto diet that everybody understands and does.

Targeted Ketogenic Diet (TKD): This variant is where you consume SKD but ingest a limited amount of fast-digesting carbohydrates before a workout.

Cyclical Ketogenic Diet (CKD): This variant of keto for bodybuilders and contests goers, usually offering one day a week to carb up and resupplies glycogen stocks.

Common Side Effects of a Keto Diet

Here are some of the more popular side effects that one comes across when people first initiate keto. Frequently the problems contribute to dehydration or loss of micronutrients (vitamins) in the body. Be sure that you're consuming enough water (close to a gallon a day) and enjoying foods containing healthy sources of micronutrients.

Cramps

Cramps (and, more importantly, leg cramps) are a fairly normal occurrence before beginning a ketogenic diet. It's typically happening in the morning or at night, but overall, it's a fairly small concern. It's a warning that there's a shortage of minerals, especially magnesium, in the body. Be sure you consume lots of fluid and eat salt on your meal. Using so will help reduce the lack of magnesium and get rid of the problem.

Constipation

The most frequent source of constipation is dehydration. An easy approach is to maximize water consumption and aim to get as close to a gallon a day as possible.

Trying to make sure veggies have some fiber. Bringing in some high-quality fiber from non-starchy vegetables will fix this issue. Though if that's not enough, normally, psyllium husk powder can work or take a probiotic.

Heart Palpitations

When switching to keto, you may find that the heart is beating both faster and slower. It's fairly normal, so don't think about it. If the condition remains, make sure that you're consuming enough liquids and eating enough salt. Usually, this is adequate to get rid of the issue right away. Though if the problem continues, it might be worth having a potassium supplement once a day.

Reduced Physical Performance

You can have some restrictions on your results when you start a keto diet, but it's generally only from your body transitioning to using fat, when your body changes in utilizing fat for energy, all of your power and stamina will return to normal. If you still notice issues with results, you can see benefits from taking carbs before exercising (or cycling carbs).

Saving Money and Budgeting

A popular myth is that the ketogenic diet is more costly than most diets out there. And, though it can be a little bit more costly than eating grain-stuffed goods, it's still better than many people believe. A ketogenic diet can be more costly than a regular American diet, but it's no different than most clean eating lifestyles. That said, there are always several ways to save money when cooking keto. The key strategies to raise money are the same as in all other budgeting:

Look for offers. There's still a discount or an offer to be had on keto-friendly products out there. Usually, you can find substantial discounts in magazines and newspapers that are delivered to your home, but they can also be paired with in-store specials and manager cuts. As paired, you will save a large portion of your keto groceries.

Bulk purchase and cook. If you're somebody who doesn't want to invest a lot of time in the kitchen, this is the best in all worlds. Buying the food at volume (specifically from wholesalers) will reduce the cost per pound immensely. Plus, you can make ahead food (bulk cook chicken thighs for pre-made beef, or cook whole meals) that are used as leftovers, meaning you waste less time preparing.

Do stuff yourself. Although it's incredibly easy to purchase certain products pre-made or pre-cooked, it still contributes to the price per pound of goods. Try prepping vegetables ahead of time instead of getting pre-cut ones. Try having your stew meat from a chuck roast. Or attempt to produce your mayo and salad dressings at home. The easiest of items will operate to cut back on your overall food shopping.

How to Reach Ketosis

Achieving ketosis is fairly simple, but it may appear complex and overwhelming for all of the details out there. Here's the bottom line about what you need to do, arranged in stages of importance:

Restrict the sugars: Many people prefer to only rely only on net carbohydrates. If you want better outcomes, restrict both. Aim to remain below 20g net carbs and below 35g gross carbs a day.

Restrict the protein consumption: Some people come over to keto from an Atkins diet and don't restrict their protein. Too much protein can contribute to lower levels of ketosis. Ideally, you ought to eat between 0.6g and 0.8g protein per pound of lean body fat. To assist with this, try using the keto calculator >

Stop thinking about fat: Fat is the main source of calories on keto – just be sure you're giving the body plenty of it. You should not lose weight on keto by malnutrition.

Drink water: Aim to drink a gallon of water a day. Make sure that you're hydrating and remaining compliant with the volume of water you consume. It not only helps regulate many important bodily functions, but it also helps manage hunger levels.

Stop snacking: Weight reduction seems to perform well because you have fewer insulin surges during the day. Unnecessary snacking can lead to stalls or delays in development.

Start fasting: Fasting can be a perfect tool to raise ketone levels reliably during the day. There are several different ways to go about it. Add workout in. It's a proven reality that exercise is safer. If you want to get the best out of your ketogenic diet, try putting in 20-30 minutes of workout a day. Also, only a short stroll will help control weight loss and blood sugar levels.

Begin supplementing: Although not normally required, supplementing can aid with a ketogenic diet.

What the Science Tell Us about the Keto Diet

The keto diet has been used to better treat epilepsy, a condition marked by seizures, for more than 100 years. More current trials are investigating the keto diet as an effective nutritional therapy for obesity and diabetes. Clinical results on the effects of the keto diet on these health problems are exceedingly minimal. Studies on the success of the keto diet are performed with limited groups of participants. And, much of the research on Alzheimer's disease depends on testing conducted on experimental animals. To completely evaluate the protection of this eating style, further study is required. Plus, research must be performed on the long-term health implications of the keto diet. Body mass index and human metabolic rates affect how easily various people generate ketones. This suggests that certain individuals lose weight more slowly with the keto diet than others even though they are pursuing the same keto diet schedule. For this community of individuals, the keto diet may be stressful and can affect their enthusiasm for making healthy lifestyle improvements. Plus, many individuals are not willing to continue with the keto diet and gain back weight after adjusting to their former eating style.

Chapter 2: Keto Diet Breakfast Recipes

Keto Hot Chocolate

YIELDS: 1

TOTAL TIME: 0 HOURS **20** MINS.

INGREDIENTS

- • 2 Tbsp. of cocoa powder, and more for flavor
- • 2 1/2 Tsp. of sugar keto (diet), (such as swerve)
- • 1 1/4 c. of Water
- • 1/4 c. of heavy cream
- • 1/4 Tsp. of Pure vanilla bean paste
- • Whipped serum, for serving

DIRECTIONS

1. In a small saucepan over medium-low heat, whisk together swerve, cocoa powder or about 2 Tbs. water until smooth and dissolved. Increase heat to medium, add remaining water and cream, and whisk until cook.

2. Mix the chocolate then pour into cup. Serve with whipped cream and a dusting of sugar powder.

Keto Sausage Breakfast Sandwich

YIELDS: 3

TOTAL TIME: 0 HOURS 15 MINS

INGREDIENTS

- 6 large size eggs
- 2 Tbsp. of heavy cream
- Pinch of red chili flakes
- Salt (kosher)
- Finely roasted black pepper
- 1 Tbsp. of butter
- 3 slices of cheddar
- 6 packaged of sausage burgers, cooked as per box directions
- Avocado, sliced

DIRECTIONS

1. Take a small bowl beat eggs, red chili flakes and heavy cream jointly. Season with pepper and salt. Melt the butter in fry pan at low flame. Add around one third of eggs in to pan. Add a piece of cheese in the center or let stay for 1 minute. Roll the ends of egg in to center, filling a cheese. Take out from heat and continue with leftover egg.

2. Serve eggs in 2 sausage buns with avocado.

Keto Breakfast Cups

YIELDS: 12

TOTAL TIME: 0 HOURS **40** MINS

INGREDIENTS

- 2 Ib. of Pork (ground)
- 1 Tbsp. thyme, finely sliced
- 2 cloves of garlic, finely chopped
- 1/2 Tsp. of Paprika
- 1/2 Tsp. of cumin, ground
- 1 Tsp. of Salt kosher
- Black pepper softly roasted
- 21/2 cup of clean minced spinach
- 1 c. of cheddar, thinly sliced
- Eggs, 12
- 1 Tbsp. of chives that are finely cut

DIRECTIONS

1. 1 Preheat the oven at 400 degrees. Combine the thyme, ground pork, paprika, garlic, salt, and cumin in a large size cup.
2. In each muffin container, add a tiny handful of pork and push up the sides to make a cup. Split the cheese and spinach equally in cups. Break the egg and add the salt and pepper on the top of each cup. Cook for around 25 minutes until the eggs are fixed and the sausage is fried.
3. Garnish and serve with chives.

Best-Ever Cabbage Hash Browns

YIELDS: 2

TOTAL TIME: 0 HOURS **25** MINS

INGREDIENTS

- 2 Large size eggs
- 1/2 Tsp. of garlic, powdered
- 1/2 Tsp. of salt (kosher)
- Freshly roasted black pepper
- 2c. of cabbage that is shredded
- ¼ of small size yellow onions, finely chopped
- 1 Tbsp. of oil (vegetable)

DIRECTIONS

1. Whisk the garlic powder, salt, and eggs together in a large cup. Add black pepper for seasoning. In egg mixture add onion and cabbage and toss to mix properly.
2. Heat oil in a large frying pan. Split the mixture in the pan into 4 patties and press spatula to soften. Cook until soft and golden, around three minutes on each side.

Chocolate Keto Protein Shake

YIELD: 1

TOTAL TIME: 0 HOURS **5** MINS

INGREDIENTS

- 3/4 c of almond milk
- 1/2 c. of ice
- 2 Tbsp. of Butter (almond)
- 2 Tbsp. of (Sugar free) powder of cocoa
- 3 Tbsp. of keto-diet sugar substitute as per taste (such as Swerve)
- 1Tbsp. seeds of chia or more for serving
- 2 Tbsp. seeds of hemp, or more for serving
- 1/2 Tbsp. of pure vanilla (extracted)
- Salt kosher as per taste

DIRECTIONS

1. Merge all of blending mixture and mix untill soft. Put into glass and serve with hemp seed and chia.

Hard Boiled Egg

YIELDS: 1

TOTAL TIME: 0 HOURS **20** MINS

INGREDIENTS

- 12 large size eggs
- Some water

DIRECTIONS

1. Place the eggs in such a wide saucepan and cover them with one inch of ice water. Keep the saucepan on the burner and get it to a boil. Immediately turn off the flame and cover the saucepan. Let settle down for eleven minutes.
2. Take it out from the pan and switch it to ice water. Until serving or peeling, let it cool for 2 minutes.

Paleo Breakfast Stacks

YIELDS: 3

TOTAL TIME: 0 HOURS **30** MINS

INGREDIENTS

- 3 sausage buns for breakfast
- 1 avocado, finely mashed
- Salt (kosher)
- Black pepper freshly roasted
- 3 large size eggs
- Chives, (for serving)
- Hot sauce, if ordered

DIRECTIONS

1. Cook the breakfast sausage as per the box's instructions.
2. Mash the avocado over the sausage for breakfast and season with pepper and salt.
3. Use cooking oil to spray the medium size pan then spray the interior of mason jar cover. Place the mason jar lid in the middle of the pan and crack the interior of an egg. Add pepper or salt and cook until the whites are set for 3 minutes, then remove the cover and begin to cook.
4. Place the egg on top of the avocado puree. Serve with chives and drizzle with your favorite spicy hot sauce.

Ham & Cheese Breakfast Roll-Ups

YIELDS: 2

TOTAL TIME: 0 HOURS **20** MINS

INGREDIENT

- 4 large size eggs
- 1/4 c of milk
- 2 Tbsp. of finely cut chives
- Salt (kosher)
- Black pepper freshly roasted
- 1Tbsp. of butter
- 1c. of cheddar shredded,(Split)
- 4 slices of ham

DIRECTIONS

1. Whisk the milk, chives, and egg together in a medium cup. Add pepper or salt.
2. Melt the butter in a medium pan over low heat. Put 1/2 of the egg mixture in the pan and shift to make a thin layer that covers the whole plan.
3. Cook for two minutes. Add1/2 cup of cheddar or seal again for 2 minutes, before the cheese has melted transfer to plate, and put 2 slices of ham or rolls them. Repeat and cook with the rest of the ingredients.

Cauliflower Toast

YIELDS: 4 - 6

TOTAL TIME: 0 HOURS **45** MINS

INGREDIENTS

- 1 cauliflower (in medium size)
- Large size egg
- 1/2 c. of cheddar cheese (shredded)
- 1Tsp.of garlic(powdered)
- Salt (kosher)
- Black pepper freshly roasted

DIRECTIONS

1. Set the oven at 425 degree temperature and cover the baking sheet with parchment paper. Finely chopped the cauliflower and switch to a large size cup. Set the microwave at high temperature for 8 minutes. Drain with cheesecloth and paper towels just before the mixture is dry.
2. In cauliflower cup, add the cheddar, garlic powder and egg and season with pepper and salt. Mix it until joint
3. Make a cauliflower into bread forms on prepared baking sheet and bake for 18 to 20 minutes until golden.
4. Switch to a plate cover with the appropriate topping, such as fried egg, mashed avocado, tomato, broccoli, and sausage.

Breakfast Bacon and Egg Salad

YIELDS: 4

TOTAL TIME: 0 HOURS **30** MINS

INGREDIENTS

Bacon vinaigrette

- 4 bacon (slices)
- 1 shallot, thinly sliced
- 3 Tbsp. of red wine(vinegar)
- 1 Tsp. of mustard (Dijon)
- 1/4 Tsp. of salt (kosher)
- 1/4 Tsp. of black pepper
- 4 Tbsp. of Oil

Salad

2 small size eggs

1 Spinach (package)

1/4 c. of crumbled feta

1 pt. of tomatoes and cherry

DIRECTIONS

1. In a large fry pan, cook the bacon. Remove the bacon slices and put on a plate and line with towel paper to drain. Implode half of the bacon until the excess fat has drained, then cut the rest of two pieces into large pieces. Set again.

2. Making the vinaigrette: Add the shallot into the pot in which the bacon has been fried, and sauté for around 1 minute over moderate flame until golden brown. Pour the shallots into a small cup and blend with the pepper, salt, red vinegar, and mustard. Whisk in the oil, and then add the crumbled bacon and blending to combine. Set again.

3. In the same pot, fried each egg and cook until the egg white is fixed.

4. Assemble the salad: Combine the feta, lettuce, tomatoes, cherry, spinach and the remaining sliced bacon in a large size dish. Cover with vinaigrette.
5. Place the salad in two cups and cover it with the fried egg. Immediately serve.

Keto Blueberry Muffins

YIELD: 1

TOTAL TIME: 0 HOURS **40** MINS

INGREDIENTS

- 2 1/2 c. of almond Flour
- 1/3 c. of Keto diet sugar (such as Swerve)
- 1 1/2 Tsp. of baking powder
- 1/2 Tsp. of baking soda
- 1/2 Tsp. salt kosher
- 1/3 c. of melted butter
- 1/3 c. of Sugar free almonds milk
- 3 large size eggs
- 1 Tsp. of pure vanilla extract
- 2/3 of c. of fresh blueberries
- ½ of lemon zest (as an option)

DIRECTIONS

1. Preheat oven to 350° and line a 12-cup muffin pan with cupcake liners.
2. In a large bowl, whisk to combine baking powder, baking soda, almond flour, salt kosher and swerve. Whisk in eggs, vanilla, almond milk, melted butter and almond milk until just together.

3. Gently fold   lemon zest (if using) and blueberries until uniformly divided. Scoop uniform quantity of butter into every cupcake liner and cook until slightly   golden brown and insert a toothpick into the middle of a muffin comes out clean, 23 minutes. Let cool slightly before presenting.

Mason Jar Omelets

YIELDS: 2

TOTAL TIME: 0 HOURS **15** MINS

INGREDIENTS

- Nonstick cooking oil
- 4 large size eggs
- 2/3 c. of cheddar shredded
- ½ of onion, thinly sliced
- 1 Chopped capsicum
- 1/2 c. of ham (sliced)
- Salt kosher
- Freshly roasted black pepper
- 1Tbsp. of Chives that are finely sliced

DIRECTIONS

1. Oil the nonstick baking spray into two liter mason jars.
2. Break two eggs into each jar. Between two jar divide the onion, ham capsicum, and cheese and season with pepper and   salt.
3. Put cover on jar and mix until eggs are scrambled and all ingredients are mixed.
4. Remove the cover and   place in the oven. Microwave for 4 minutes on low flame, and looking every 30 seconds. Garnish with chives, and serve immediately.

Keto Fat Bombs

YIELDS: 16

TOTAL TIME: 0 HOURS **30** MIN

INGREDIENTS

- 8 oz. of cream cheese, mitigated at room temp.
- 1/2 c. of keto diet (peanuts) butter
- 1/4 c of (coconut oil)
- 1/4 Tsp. of salt (kosher)
- 1/2 c. of dark chocolate (keto diet) (such as Lily's)

DIRECTIONS

1. Cover the baking sheet with a tiny parchment paper. Mix the peanut butter, salt, cream cheese and 1/4 cup of coconut oil in a medium dish. With the help of hand blender beat the mixture for around 2 minutes until all ingredients are properly mixed. Keep the dish for 10 to 15 minutes in the freezer to firm up slightly.
2. Using a tiny cookie spoon or scoop to make a Tbs. sized balls until the (peanut butter) mixture has been settled. Keep in the freezer for 5 minutes to harden.
3. Besides that, making a drizzle of chocolate: mix the cocoa powder and the leftover coconut oil in a safe microwave dish and cook for 30 seconds until completely melt. Drizzle over the balls of peanut butter and put them back in the fridge to harden for 5 minutes.
4. Keep the cover and freeze it for storage purpose.

Cloud Eggs

YIELDS: 4

TOTAL TIME: 0 HOURS **20** MINS

INGREDIENTS

- 8 large size eggs
- 1 c. of Parmesan, thinly sliced
- 1/2 lb. of Ham deli, diced
- Salt (kosher)
- Freshly made black pepper
- For serving, finely sliced chives

DIRECTIONS

1. Heat the oven at 450 °C and spread cooking oil on a large baking sheet. Separate the yolks and egg whites, yolks are keep in small cup and egg whites are keep in large cup egg whites. Use a hand blender or whisk break egg whites before stiff peaks shape and cook for 3 minutes. Fold in the ham and parmesan or season with pepper and salt.
2. Spoon the 8 mounds of egg onto the heated baking dish and indent centers to make nests. Cook for around 3 minutes, until lightly golden.
3. Spoon the egg yolk cautiously into the middle of each nest, then season with pepper or salt. Cook for around 3 minutes more until the yolks are ready.
4. Before presenting, garnish it with chives.

Chapter 3: Keto Diet Lunch Recipes

Cobb Egg Salad

YIELDS: 6

TOTAL TIME: 0 HOURS **20** MINS

INGREDIENTS

- 3 Tbsp. of mayonnaise
- 3 Tbsp. of yogurt
- 2 tbsp. of vinegar with red wine
- Salt (kosher)
- Black pepper freshly roasted
- 8 hard-boiled eggs, sliced into 8 pieces, and more for garnishing.
- 8 bacon strips, fried and crumbled, and more for garnishing.
- 1 avocado, cut finely
- 1/2 c. of blue cheese, crumbled, and more for garnishing
- 1/2 c. of halved cherry tomatoes, and more for garnishing
- 2 Tbsp. of chives that are finely chopped

DIRECTIONS

1. Mix the yogurt, red vinegar and mayonnaise together in a small cup. Seasoning with pepper and salt.
2. Mix the avocado, bacon, eggs, pineapple, cherry tomatoes and blue cheese, softly together in a large serving cup. Gently roll in the mayonnaise coating until the all ingredients are finely coated, and then sprinkle with pepper and salt.
3. Serving with chives and supplementary toppings

Taco Stuffed Avocado

YIELDS: 4 - 8

TOTAL TIME: 0 HOURS **25** MINS

INGREDIENTS

- 4 large size avocados
- 1 lime juice
- 1 Tbsp. of olive oil (extra-virgin)
- 1 medium size onion, minced
- 1 lb. minced meat of beef
- 1 taco seasoning pack
- Salt (kosher)
- Blinerack pepper freshly roasted
- 2/3 of c. of chopped Mexican cheese
- 1/2 c. of chopped Lettuce
- 1/2 c. of Grape tomatoes (Sliced)
- Sour milk, for garnishing

DIRECTIONS

1. Pit and halve the avocados halve and pit. Scoop out a bit of avocado with the help of a spoon, forming a wide layer. Dice extracted avocado and later put aside for use. Pinch the lime juice (to avoid frying!) at all the avocados.
2. Heat the oil in a medium size pan over medium heat. Add the onion and roast for around 5 minutes, until soft. Break up the meat with a wooden spatula then add ground beef and taco for seasoning. Sprinkle with pepper and salt, and roast for around 6 minutes until the beef is no more pink. Drain the fat after removing from the heat.
3. Fill up the each avocado halve with meat, then and coat with cheese, reserved avocado, tomato, onion, lettuce, and a dollop of sour cream.

Buffalo Shrimp Lettuce Wraps

YIELDS: 4

TOTAL TIME: 0 HOURS **35** MINS

INGREDIENTS

- 1/4 Tbsp. of butter
- 2 cloves of garlic, chopped
- 1/4 c. of Hot sauce, for example, Frank's
- 1 Tbsp. of olive oil (extra-virgin)
- 1 lbs. of Chopped and finely diced shrimp, tails (cut)
- Salt kosher
- Black pepper freshly roasted
- 1 head Romaine, different leaves, for garnishing
- 1/4 of red onion, finely minced
- 1 rib celery, finely chopped
- 1/2 c. of Crumbled blue cheese

DIRECTIONS

1. Making the buffalo sauce: Melt the butter in a small pan. When fully melted, then add chopped garlic and simmer for 1 minute, until golden brown. Add hot sauce and stir together. Switch the heat to low whilst the shrimp is frying.
2. Making shrimp: Heat oil in a large frying pan. Put some shrimp and sprinkle with pepper and salt. Cook, turning midway, until both sides are opaque and pink, around 2 minutes on each side. Turn off the flame and add the (buffalo) sauce and toss to fill.
3. Prepare wraps: In the middle of the romaine leaf add a little scoop of shrimp, then coat with celery, blue cheese and red onion.

Keto Broccoli Salad

YIELDS: 4

TOTAL TIME: 0 HOURS **35** MINS

INGREDIENTS

For the salad:

- Salt (kosher)
- 3 broccoli heads, sliced into bite-size parts
- 1/2 c. of cheddar shredded
- 1/4 red onion, finely cut
- 1/4 c. of   almonds sliced (baked)
- 3 bacon slices, fried and crumbled
- 2 Tbsp. of Chives that are finely cut

For the dressing:

- 2/3 of c. of mayonnaise
- 3 Tbsp. of   Vinegar (Apple Cider)
- 1 Tbsp. of Mustard dijon
- salt kosher
- Black pepper freshly roasted

DIRECTIONS

1. Bring the 6 cups of (salted) water to a boil in a medium pot or frying pan. Prepare a big bowl of ice water while waiting for the water to heat.
2. Put some broccoli florets to the boiling water and simmer for 1 to 2 minutes, until soft. Detach with a slotted spoon,   and put in the prepared ice water cup. Drain the florets in a colander while it is cold.
3. In a medium dish, whisk together the ingredients for the dressing. Season with pepper and salt to taste.
4. In a large bowl, combine all the salad ingredients and pour over the coating. Toss before the components are coated in the dressing. Refrigerate until prepared

Keto Bacon Sushi

YIELDS: 12

TOTAL TIME: 0 HOURS **30** MINS

INGREDIENTS

- 6 bacon pieces, (halved)
- 2 Persian cucumbers, cut finely
- 2 medium size carrots, cut finely
- 1 avocado, in slices
- 4 oz. of melted cream cheese, (cooked)

DIRECTIONS

1. Preheat oven to 400 ° degrees. Cover a baking sheet and match it with a cooling rack and aluminum foil. Put some bacon pieces in an even layer and cook for 11 to 13 minutes until mildly crisp but still pliable.
2. Mean a while, cut avocado, cucumbers, and broccoli into pieces around the width of bacon.
3. Spread an equal layer of cream cheese on each slice until the bacon is cold enough to touch it. Split up the vegetables between the bacon uniformly and put them on one side. Tightly roll up the vegetables.
4. Serve and garnish with sesame seeds.

Keto Burger Fat Bombs

YIELDS: 20

TOTAL TIME: 0 HOURS **30** MINS

INGREDIENTS

- Cooking oil
- 1 lbs. of ground-based meat
- 1/2 Tsp. of Powdered garlic
- Salt Kosher
- Black pepper freshly roasted
- 2 Tbsp. of cold butter,20 (sliced)
- 2 oz. of cheddar cheese 20 (sliced)
- Lettuce berries, meant for garnishing
- For garnishing, finely sliced tomatoes
- Mustard, for garnishing

DIRECTIONS

1. Preheat the oven at 375 °C and oil mini muffin container with cooking oil. And season the beef with garlic powder, salt, and pepper in a medium dish.
2. In the bottom of each muffin tin cup add the 1 Tsp. of beef equally, and fully covering the bottom. Place a layer of butter on top and add 1 Tsp. of beef over the butter to fully cover.
3. In each cup, place a slice of cheddar on top of the meat and place the remaining beef over the cheese to fully cover.
4. Bake for about 15 minutes, before the meat is ready. Let wait until cool.
5. Using a metal offset spoon carefully to release each burger out of the tin. Serve with salad leaves, mustard and onions.

Keto Taco Cups

YIELDS: 1 DOZEN

TOTAL TIME: 0 HOURS **30** MINS

INGREDIENTS

- 2 c. of Cheddar (Sliced) cheese
- 1 Tbsp. of Olive Oil (extra-Virgin)
- 1 small size chopped onion
- 3 cloves of garlic , finely chopped
- 1 lbs. of meat, ground
- 1 Tsp. of chili(in powdered form)
- 1/2 Tsp. of Cumin ,ground
- 1/2 tsp. of Paprika
- Salt (kosher)
- Black pepper freshly roasted
- Sour cream, to serve
- Diced avocado, planned for serving
- Cilantro finely chopped, for serving
- Tomatoes, chopped, for garnishing

DIRECTIONS

1. Preheat the oven to 375 ° and use parchment paper to cover a wide baking sheet. Add 2 teaspoons of cheddar a half inch away. Cook for around 6 minutes, until creamy and the edges begin to turn golden. Leave the baking sheet for a minute until cool.
2. Besides that, apply the oil in the muffin tin bottom with a cooking spray, then carefully pick up the slices of melted cheese and put them on the muffin tin bottom. Add another inverted muffin container until cool for 10 minutes. Using your hands to help shape the cheese around the twisted pan because you do not have a second muffin tin.
3. Preheat the large size pan over medium heat. Put the onion and simmer for around 5 minutes, mixing frequently, until soft. Whisk in the garlic, then add the ground beef to break up the beef with the help of wooden spoon. Cook for around 6 minutes, until the beef is no longer pink, and then drain the fat.
4. Place the meat back in the pan and season with cumin, chili powder, cinnamon, paprika, and pepper.
5. Move the cups of cheese into a serving bowl. Cover it with cooked ground beef and serve with cilantro, sour cream, tomatoes, and avocado.

Copycat Chicken Lettuce Wraps

YIELDS: 4

TOTAL TIME: 0 HOURS **30** MINS

INGREDIENTS

- 3 Tbsp. of Sauce (Hoisin)
- 2 Tbsp. Soy sauce (low-sodium)
- 2 Tbsp. vinegar from rice wine
- 1 Tbsp. of sriracha (as an option)
- 1 Tsp. oil with sesame seeds
- 1 Tbsp. olive oil (extra-virgin)
- 1 medium size chopped onion
- 2 cloves of garlic, chopped
- 1 Tbsp. of freshly coated ginger
- 1 lbs. of Chicken, ground
- 1/2 c. of drained and diced canned water chestnuts
- 2 green onions, cut finely
- Salt kosher
- Black pepper freshly roasted
- Large leafy lettuce for serving (leaves separated),
- Fried white rice, for garnishing(as an option)

DIRECTIONS

1. Making a sauce: Whisk together the soya sauce, the hoisin sauce, the sriracha the rice wine vinegar, the Sriracha and the sesame oil in a tiny cup.
2. Heat the olive oil in a large pan over a medium-high heat. Put some onions and cook for 5 minutes until soft, then stir the garlic and ginger and cook for 1 more minute until golden brown. Add ground chicken and cook until the meat is opaque and mostly finished, trying to break up the meat with a wooden spoon.

3. Add the sauce and simmer again for 1 or 2 minutes, before the sauce is slightly reduced and the chicken is thoroughly cooked. Switch off the flame, add green onions and chestnuts and mix. Season with pepper and salt.

4. Spoon rice and add a big scoop of chicken mixture (about 1/4 cup) into the middle of each lettuce leaf (if used). Instantly serve

Egg Roll Bowls

YIELDS: 4

TOTAL TIME: 0 HOURS **35** MINS

INGREDIENTS

- 1 Tbsp. of oil for vegetables
- 1 clove of garlic, chopped
- 1 Tbsp. fresh ginger chopped
- 1 lbs. of pork, ground
- 1 Tbsp. of oil with sesame seeds
- 1/2 onion, cut finely
- 1 c. of Carrot(sliced)
- 1/4 green, thinly sliced (cabbage)
- 1/4 c. of soya sauce
- 1 Tbsp. of sriracha
- 1 small size green onion, finely chopped
- 1 Tbsp. of sesame seeds

DIRECTIONS

1. Heat the vegetable oil in a large skillet over medium heat. Add the garlic and ginger and roast for 1 to 2 minutes until it is moist. Add pork and roast until there is no more pink color has been shown.

2. Place the pork and add the sesame oil to other side. Add the tomato, cabbage, and potato. Add the soy sauce and Sriracha and whisk to combine with the beef. Cook for 5 to 8 minutes, until the cabbage is soft.

3. Garnish with sesame seeds and green onions and shift the mixture to a serving bowl. Serve immediately.

Caprese Zoodles

YIELDS: 4

TOTAL TIME: 0 HOURS **25** MINS

INGREDIENTS

- 4 large size zucchinis
- 2 Tbsp. of olive oil (extra-virgin)
- Kosher salt
- Black pepper freshly roasted
- 2 c. of cherry tomatoes, sliced in half
- 1 c. of mozzarella cubes, cut into pieces(if large)
- 1/4 c. fresh leaves of basil
- 2 Tbsp. of vinegar (balsamic)
- DIRECTIONS

1. Using a spiralizer, make zoodles with the help of zucchini.
2. In a large cup, add the zoodles mix with the olive oil, and add pepper and salt. Let them marinate for 15 minutes.
3. Add the basil, peppers, and mozzarella in zoodles and toss until mixed.
4. Drizzle and serve with balsamic.

Best-Ever Keto Quesadillas

YIELDS: 4

TOTAL TIME: 0 HOURS **35** MINS

INGREDIENTS

- 1 Tbsp. of olive oil (extra-virgin)
- 1 chopped bell pepper
- 1/2of onion(yellow), chopped
- 1/2 Tsp. of chili powdered
- Salt kosher
- Black pepper freshly roasted
- 3 c. of Monterey jack shredded
- 3 c. of cheddar cheese, shredded
- 4 c. of Chicken shredded
- 1 avocado, cut thinly
- 1 green onion, finely chopped
- Sour cream, for serving

DIRECTIONS

1. Preheat the oven to 400C and cover the parchment paper with two medium size baking sheets.
2. Heat the oil in a medium saucepan over medium heat. Season with salt, chili powder and pepper and add onion and pepper. Cook for 5 minutes, until it is tender. Transfer to a dish.
3. In a medium cup, mix the cheeses together. In the middle of both prepared baking sheets, add 1 1/2 cups of cheese mixture. Spread into an even coat and form the size of a flour tortilla into a circle.
4. Bake the cheeses for 8 to 10 minutes before they are melted and slightly golden along the sides. Add one half of   avocado slices, onion-pepper mixture, shredded chicken and avocado slices. Let it cool slowly, then use the small spoon and parchment paper and carefully fold and lift one end of the cheese

"tortilla" over the end with the topping. Return to the oven to heat for an extra 3 to 4 minutes. To make 2 more quesadillas, repeat the procedure.

5. Split each quesadilla into quarters. Before serving, garnish it with sour cream and green onion.

Cheeseburger Tomatoes

YIELDS: 4

TOTAL TIME: 0 HOURS **20** MINS

INGREDIENTS

- 1 Tbsp. of olive oil (extra-virgin)
- 1 medium size onion, minced
- 2 cloves of garlic, chopped
- 1 lbs. of ground-based meat
- 1 Tbsp. of ketchup
- 1 Tbsp. of mustard (Yellow)
- 4 sliced tomatoes
- Salt kosher
- Black paper freshly roasted
- 2/3 of c. of cheddar shredded
- 1/4 c. of Iceberg lettuce shredded
- 4 coins with pickles
- Seeds of sesame, for garnishing

DIRECTIONS

1. Heat oil in a medium pan over medium heat. Add the onion and cook for approximately 5 minutes until soft, then add the garlic. Add the ground beef, split up the meat with a wooden spoon and roast for around 6 minutes until the beef is no longer pink. Drain fats. Season with pepper and salt, then add the ketchup and mustard.

2. Because they are stem-side out, tossing tomatoes. Cut the tomatoes into six slices and be cautious not to cut the tomatoes full. Fold the slices carefully. Divide the tomatoes equally with the cooked ground beef, then fill it with lettuce and cheese.
3. Add sesame seeds and pickle coins for flavoring.

No-Bread Italian Subs

YIELDS: 6

TOTAL TIME: 0 HOURS **15** MINS

INGREDIENTS

- 1/2 c. of mayonnaise
- 2 Tbsp. of Vinegar with red wine
- 1 Tbsp. olive oil (extra-virgin)
- 1 tiny clove of garlic, finely chopped
- 1 Tsp. of seasoning (Italian)
- 6 slices of ham
- 12 salami sliced
- 12 pepperoni, sliced
- 6 provolone slices
- 1 c. of romaine(chopped)
- 1/2 c. of red peppers (roasted)

DIRECTIONS

1. Making a smooth Italian dressing: whisk the mustard, mayonnaise, garlic, oil, and Italian seasoning together in a small bowl until they are mixed.
2. Prepare the sandwiches: Layer a pieces of pork, two pieces of pepperoni, two pieces of salami and a piece of provolone.
3. In the center, add a handful of Romaine and a few roasted red peppers. Drizzle, with fluffy Italian sauce, then roll up and eat. Continue the procedure with the rest of the ingredients until you have 6 roll-ups.

California Burger Bowls

YIELDS: 4

TOTAL TIME: 0 HOURS **20** MINS

INGREDIENTS

For the dressing:

- 1/2 c. of olive oil (extra-virgin)
- 1/3 c. of vinegar (balsamic)
- 3Tbsp. of mustard dijon
- 2 Tsp. of. honey
- 1 clove of garlic , chopped
- Salt kosher
- Black pepper freshly roasted

For the burger:

- 1 lbs. of grass fed organic ground beef
- 1 Tsp. of Sauce (worcestershire)
- 1/2 tsp. of chili Powdered
- 1/2 tsp. onion Powdered
- Salt kosher
- Black pepper freshly roasted
- 1 packet of butter head lettuce
- 1 medium size red onion, sliced (¼)
- 1 avocado,(in pieces)
- 2 Walmart medium size tomato, thinly sliced

DIRECTIONS

1. Making the dressing: Whisk together the dressing components in a medium dish.
2. Making burgers: Mix beef with chili powder, (Worcestershire) sauce and onion powder in another large bowl. Season with salt and pepper and whisk until blend. Shape into 4 patties.

3. Heat a wide grill pan over medium heat and grill the onions until they are crispy and soft, around 3 minutes on at each end. Remove the grill from the pan and add the burgers. Bake until browned and fried to your taste on all ends, around 4 minutes per end for medium.

4. Assemble: Toss the lettuce with 1/2 of the dressing in a wide bowl and split between 4 bowls. Cover each with a patty of steak, tomatoes, fried onions, slices of 1/4 avocado. Drizzle and serve with the remaining dressing.

Chapter 4: Dinner Recipes

Keto Corned Beef & Cabbage

TOTAL TIME: 5 HOURS 0 MINS

YIELDS: 6

INGREDIENTS:

- 3 to 4 1bs. of corned beef
- Onions, 2 (quartered)
- 4 stalks of, quartered crosswise celery
- 1 pack of pickling spices
- Salt (Kosher)
- Black Pepper
- 1 medium size cabbage (green), sliced into 2 wedges
- carrots (2), sliced and split into 2" part
- 1/2 c. of Dijon mustard
- 2 Tbsp. of (apple cider) vinegar
- 1/4 c. of mayonnaise
- 2 Tbsp. capers, finely sliced, plus 1 tsp. of brine
- 2 Tbsp. of parsley, finely cut

Directions:

1. Place corned beef, onion, celery, and pickling spices into a large pot. Add the water to cover by 2", salt with season or Pepper, and bring to the boil. Medium heat, cover, and Simmer very (tender), 3–3 1/2 hours.
2. In the meantime, whisk Dijon mustard and apple cider vinegar in a small bowl and add salt and pepper. And in another bowl, mix capers, mayo, caper brine, and parsley. Season with salt and pepper

3. Added carrots and cabbage continue cooking for 45 minutes to 1 hour more until cabbage is soft. Remove meat, cabbage, and carrots from the pot. Piece of corned beef and season with a little more pepper and salt.
4. Present with both sauces on the side for soaking.

Keto Fried Chicken:

TOTAL TIME: 1 HOUR 15 MINS

YIELDS: 6 - 8

INGREDIENTS

FOR THE CHICKEN

- 6 (Bone-in), chicken breasts with skin, about 4 lbs.
- Salt (Kosher)
- Black Pepper, ground and fresh
- 2 large size eggs
- 1/2 c. of heavy cream
- 3/4 c. of almond flour
- 1 1/2 c. perfectly crushed pork rinds
- 1/2 c. of grated Parmesan, fresh
- 1 Tsp. of Garlic in powder form
- 1/2 Tsp. of paprika

FOR THE SPICY MAYO:

- 1/2 c. of Mayonnaise
- 1 1/2 Tsp. of Hot sauce

DIRECTIONS

1. Preheat oven to 400° and cover a wide baking sheet with parchment paper. Pat dry chicken with paper towels and add salt and pepper.

2. In a small bowl, mix together eggs and heavy cream. In another small dish, mix almond flour, pork rinds, Parmesan, garlic powder, and paprika. Add salt and black pepper.
3. Work at one time, soak the chicken in egg mix, then in the almonds flour mix, pressing to cover. Put the chicken on the lined baking dish.
4. Bake till chicken is gold and internal temp exceeds 165°, about 45 minutes.
5. In the meantime, produce dipping sauce: In a medium dish, mix mayonnaise and hot sauce. Add more hot sauce based on desired spiciness amount.
6. Serve chicken warm with dipping sauce.

Garlic Rosemary Pork Chops:

TOTAL TIME: 0 HOURS 30 MINS
YIELDS: 4
INGREDIENTS:
- 4 pieces of pork loin
- Salt (kosher)
- Black pepper freshly roasted
- 1Tbsp. of Freshly chopped rosemary
- 2 Garlic cloves, minced
- 1/2 c (1 stick) of butter melted
- 1 Tbsp. of Extra-virgin (olive oil)

DIRECTIONS:

1. Preheat the oven to 375 degrees. With salt and black pepper, season the pork chops generously.
2. Mix the honey, rosemary, and garlic together in a shallow dish. Only put back.
3. Heat the olive oil in an oven-safe skillet over (medium-high) heat and add the pork chops. Sear until golden for 4 minutes, flip and bake for a further 4 minutes. Pork chops are appropriately coated with garlic butter for 10-12 minutes.
4. Add more garlic butter to serve.

Keto Bacon Sushi

TOTAL TIME: 0 HOURS 30 MINS

YIELDS: 12

INGREDIENTS:

- 6 bacon strips, cut in half
- 2 cucumbers (Persian), cut thin
- 2 carrots (medium), cut thinly
- 1 (avocado), in slices
- 4 oz. (Creamy) cheese, cooked, soft
- Seeds of sesame (garnish)

DIRECTIONS:

1. Preheat the oven to 400 degrees. Line a baking sheet and match with a (cooling rack) with (aluminum) foil. Lay bacon half with an even surface and cook for 11 to 13 minutes unless mildly crispy but always pliable.
2. In the meantime, split the bacon's size into pieces of cucumbers, broccoli, and avocado.
3. Spread an equal surface of cream cheese from each strip until the bacon is cold enough to touch it. Divide the vegetables into the bacon equally and put them in one hand. Strictly roll up the vegetables.
4. Season with and serve the sesame seeds.

Keto Chicken Parmesan

TOTAL TIME: 0 HOURS 55 MINS

YIELDS: 4

INGREDIENTS:

- 4 boneless without skin breasts of chicken
- Kosher salt
- 1c. of Almond Flour
- 3 big, beaten eggs
- 3 c. of Parmesan, freshly grated, and much more for serving
- 2 Tsp. of Powdered garlic
- 1 1/2 c. of Mozzarella Sliced
- 1 Tsp. of onion in powdered form
- 2 Tsp. of Oregano dried
- Oil for vegetables
- 3/4 c. Sugar-free, low-carb tomato sauce
- Fresh leaves of basil for topping

DIRECTIONS

1. Preheat the oven to 400 degrees. Halve the chicken breasts crosswise with a sharp knife. Season the chicken with salt and pepper on both sides.
2. Put the almond flour and eggs in 2 different shallow cups. Combine the parmesan, garlic (powder), onion (powder), and oregano in the third shallow dish. With salt and pepper, season.
3. Dip the chicken cutlets into the almond flour, then the eggs, the Parmesan mixture, and push to cover.
4. Heat 2 teaspoons of oil in a large skillet. Add chicken and roast, 2 to 3 minutes on each hand, until golden and cooked through. Function as required in batches, inserting more oil as appropriate.

5. Move the fried cutlets to a 9-inch-x-13-inch baking dish, distribute the tomato sauce uniformly over each cutlet, and finish with the mozzarella.
6. Bake for 10 to 12 minutes before the cheese melts. If needed, broil for 3 minutes until the cheese is golden.
7. Until eating, top with basil and more Parmesan.

Tuscan Butter Shrimp

TOTAL TIME: 0 HOURS 55 MINS

YIELDS: 4

INGREDIENTS

- 2 tbsp. of olive oil extra-virgin
- 1 lb. deveined, peeled, lobster and tails cut
- salt (kosher)
- Black pepper freshly roasted
- 3 tbsp. of Butter
- 3 garlic cloves, minced
- 1 1/2 c. of halved tomatoes with cherry
- 3 c. of spinach for kids
- 1/2 c. of heavy cream
- 1/4 c. of Parmesan, finely grated
- 1/4 c. of thinly cut basil
- Lemon wedges meant for serving as an option

DIRECTIONS

1. Heat oil in a frying pan over medium heat. Season the shrimp with salt and pepper all over. Add the shrimp and sear until the underside is golden, around 2 minutes, and then turn until opaque, until the oil is shimmering but still not burning. Remove and set aside from the skillet.
2. Lower the heat to mild and add some butter. When the butter is melted, stir in the garlic and simmer for around 1 minute, until fragrant. Sprinkle with salt and

substitute the cherry tomatoes. Cook until the tomatoes start to burst, then add the spinach and cook until the spinach begins to wilt.

3. Stir in the heavy cream, basil and parmesan cheese and carry the mixture to a boil. Reduce the heat to low and boil for around 3 minutes before the sauce is significantly reduced.

4. Place the shrimp back in the pan and mix to blend. Cook unless shrimp is cooked through, garnish with more basil, and squeeze lemon on top before eating.

Zoodle Alfredo with Bacon

TOTAL TIME: 0 HOURS 20 MINS

YIELDS: 4

INGREDIENTS:

- 1/2 lb. of Chopped bacon
- 1 minced shallot,
- 2 garlic cloves, minced
- 1/4 c. of Black Alcohol, White Wine
- 1 1/2 c. of heavy cream
- 1/2 c. of Parmesan(cheese) grated, but mostly for garnishing
- 1 pack of zucchini (noodles) (16 oz.)
- Kosher Salt
- Black pepper freshly roast

DIRECTIONS

1. Cook the bacon until crisp, 8 minutes, in a wide saucepan over medium heat. Drain it on a tray lined with paper towels.

2. Pour all but 2 teaspoons of (bacon); then shallots are included. Cook until tender, around 2 minutes, and then add garlic and cook for about 30 seconds until it is fragrant. Add wine and cook before half the quantity is depleted.

3. Connect the heavy cream to the mixture and get it to a boil. Lower the flame and stir in the Parmesan cheese. Cook for about 2 minutes, until the sauce, has thick

somewhat. Add the zucchini (noodles) and toss in the sauce until thoroughly covered. Take the heat off and stir in the fried bacon.

Keto Chicken Soup

TOTAL TIME: 1 HOUR 0 MINS

YIELDS: 4 - 6

INGREDIENTS:

- 2 tbsp. Oil for vegetables
- 1 medium onion, minced
- 5 garlic cloves, crushed
- 2" Fresh ginger bit, sliced
- 1 tiny cauliflower, sliced into florets
- 3/4 Tsp. smashed flakes of red pepper
- 1 medium carrot, on a bias, peeled and thin slices
- 6 c. low-sodium broth of poultry
- 1 celery stem, thinly sliced
- 2 skinless, boneless breasts of chicken
- For garnish, finely cut parsley

DIRECTIONS

1. Heat oil in a big pot over low heat. Add the carrot, ginger, and garlic. Cook before the browning stops.
2. In the meantime, pulse cauliflower before it is split into rice-sized granules in a food processor. Return the cauliflower to the pot with the onion mixture and cook for around 8 minutes over medium-high heat until golden.
3. Bring to a boil and incorporate pepper flakes, onions, celery and chicken (broth). Add the chicken breasts and cook gently for around 15 minutes before they hit a temp of 165 ° C. Remove from the pan, leave to cool and shred until cool enough

to treat. Meanwhile, proceed to cook, 3 to 5 minutes more, until the vegetables are soft.

4. Apply the (Shredded) chicken back to the broth and cut the ginger from the bath. Season with salt and pepper to taste, then garnish before serving with parsley.

Foil Pack Grilled Salmon with Lemony Asparagus

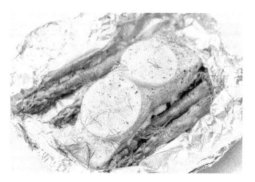

TOTAL TIME: 0 HOURS **20** MINS

YIELDS: 4

INGREDIENTS:

- 20 spears of asparagus, cut
- 4 6-oz. Skin-on fillets of salmon
- 4Tbsp. of Butter, break
- 2 lemons, cut
- Kosher salt
- Black pepper freshly roasted
- Broken dill (fresh), for season

DIRECTIONS:

1. On a hard floor lie two bits of foil. Put on the foil five spears of asparagus and finish with a salmon fillet, 1 tablespoon of butter, and two lemon slices. Cover loosely, and repeat for the rest of the ingredients and you'll have a limit of four sets.
2. High Heat Barbecue. To fry and barbecue, apply foil packets until salmon is cook through and asparagus is soft for about 10 minutes.
3. Sprinkle and mix with dill.

Garlicky Shrimp Zucchini Pasta

TOTAL TIME: 1 HOUR 50 MINS

YIELDS: 4

INGREDIENTS

- 1/4 c. Of olive oil extra-virgin
- 1/4 c. the Juice in Lemons
- Kosher (salt)
- 1 head (cauliflower), cut leaves and trimmed stem such that cauliflower lies flat but still intact
- 1 (10-oz.) box of frozen (spinach), thawed, stretched out and sliced with water
- 2 big, beaten eggs
- 4 green onions, cut thinly
  - 2 cloves of garlic, minced
  - 3/4 c. of cheddar Shredded
  - 4 oz. of soft and cube white cheese
  - 1/2 c. panko a panko
  - 1/4 c. of parmesan Rubbed
  - 1 lb. of bacon thinly cut

DIRECTIONS

1. Preheat the oven to 450 degrees. In a big kettle, put eight cups of water, oil, lemon juice and 2 tablespoons of salt to a boil. Add the cauliflower and get it to a simmer again. To hold it submerged, reduce it to a gentle simmer and put a plate on top of the cauliflower. Simmer for around 12 minutes before a knife is quickly inserted into the middle.
2. Transfer the cauliflower to a narrow rimmed baking sheet using 2 slotted spoons or a mesh spider. Only let it cool.
3. In the meanwhile, add lettuce (eggs, green onions, garlic, cheddar, cream cheese, panko, and parmesan cheese) and placed a 3⁄4-inch tip in a piping bag.
4. Place on a rimmed baking sheet with cooled cauliflower stem side up. Pipe filling of florets between stalks. Flip down the side of the cauliflower stem, and then

spread bacon strips, only slightly overlapping strips, over the cauliflower, tucking strip ends into the cauliflower bottom.

5. Roast, halfway through the spinning pan, before golden all over, maybe 30 minutes.

Cajun Parmesan Salmon

TOTAL TIME: 0 HOURS 45 MINS

YIELDS: 4

INGREDIENTS:

- 1 tbsp. Olive oil (extra-virgin)
- 4 (4-oz.) Salmon fillets (preferably wild)
- 2 Tsp. Seasoning the Cajun
- 2 Tbsp. of Butter
- 3 garlic cloves, minced
- 1/3 c. Low-sodium(chicken) or soup with vegetables
- Juice of 1 lemon
- 1 Tbsp. of honey
- 1 Tbsp. Freshly sliced parsley, with more for garnishing
- 2Tbsp. Parmesan, finely chopped
- Slices of lemon, for serving

DIRECTIONS

1. Heat oil in a frying pan over medium heat. Season the salmon with 1 tsp. of Cajun pepper and seasoning, then apply the skin-side-up to the skillet. Cook the salmon for around 6 minutes before it is intensely brown, then turn and cook for 2 more minutes. Transfer to a dish.
2. To the skillet, apply butter and garlic. Stir in the Broth, lemon juice, sugar, remaining Cajun seasoning teaspoon (parsley), and parmesan when the butter has melted. Take the combination to a boil.

3. Lower the heat to mild and return the salmon to the skillet. Simmer for 3 or 4 more minutes before the sauce is decreased, and the salmon is fried.
4. Apply slices of lemon to the pan and eat.

Beef Tenderloin:

TOTAL TIME: 1 HOUR **50** MINS

YIELDS: 4

INGREDIENTS

FOR BEEF:

- 1/2 c. Olive oil (extra-virgin)
- 2 Tbsp. Vinegar (Balsamic)
- 2 Tbsp. Mustard, whole grain
- Thyme(fresh), 3 sprigs
- 3 rosemary sprigs, fresh
- 1 bay leaf
- 2 garlic cloves, crushed
- 2 tbsp. of honey
- 1 (2-lb.) tenderloin beef
- 1 Tsp. salt, Kosher
- 1 Tsp. Black pepper, roasted, fresh
- 1 Tsp. The Dried(Rosemary)
- 1 garlic clove, minced

- **SAUCE FOR YOGURT**

- 1/2 c. Yogurt (Greek)
- 1/4 c. Sour milk, sour cream
- 1 Tsp. Horseradish prepared
- 1/2 lemon extract
- Kosher salt

DIRECTIONS

1. Mix the vinegar, oil, thyme, mustard, rosemary, crushed garlic, bay leaf, and honey together in a wide container. Return the meat to the package, cover with plastic wrap, and marinate for 1 hour or up to one day in the refrigerator. Optional: Before frying, get the tenderloin to room temperature.
2. Preheat the oven to around 450C. Line an aluminum foil rimmed baking sheet and fit a wire rack inside. Strip the marinade from the tenderloin and wipe it dry with paper towels. Add salt, pepper, rosemary, and minced garlic to season all over and put on the rack.
3. Roast until baked to your taste, around 20 minutes for special occasions. Until slicing, let it rest for 5 to 10 minutes.
4. Meanwhile, render the sauce: whisk the milk, sour cream, horseradish and lemon juice together in a medium container, and season with salt.
5. Slice the tenderloin and eat it on the side with sauce.

Baked Cajun Salmon

TOTAL TIME: 0 HOURS 30 MINS

YIELDS: 4

INGREDIENTS

- 1/2 large size white onion, cut thinly
- bell pepper (red), cut thinly
- 1 thinly cut orange bell pepper
- cloves of thinly sliced garlic
- Salt (kosher)
- Black Pepper, fresh, ground
- Three Tbsp. of Olive Oil (Extra-Virgin)
- 1 Tbsp. of thyme in dry form
- 1 Tbsp. of seasoning (Cajun)
- 2 Tsp. Of tweet paprika

- Tsp. of powdered garlic
- 6-oz. Filets of Salmon

DIRECTIONS:

1. Preheat the oven to 400 degrees. Stir in the onions, pepper and garlic on a   broad baking dish. Season with pepper and salt and toss with gasoline.
2. Prepare a spice mix: mix together thyme, Cajun seasoning, and paprika and garlic powder in a small cup.
3. On a baking sheet, put the salmon, top the bits with the seasoning mixture and rub them all over the salmon.
4. Bake for 20 minutes until the vegetables and salmon are soft and cooked properly.

Chapter 5: Deserts and Snacks Recipes

Keto Sugar-Free Cheesecake

TOTAL TIME: 8 HOURS 0 MINS

YIELDS: 8 - 10

INGREDIENTS:

- 1/2 c. of almond flour
- 1/2 c. Flour of coconut
- 1/4 c. of coconut, shredded
- 1/2 c. (1 stick) of melted butter
- 3 (8-oz.) cream cheese blocks, soft to room temp
- 16 oz. of sour cream (room temperature)
- 1 Tbsp. of stevia
- 2 Tsp. a sample of pure vanilla
- 3 large size eggs, at room temperature
- Strawberries, diced, for serving

DIRECTIONS

1. Heat the oven to 300 degrees. Create the crust: Oil a spring pan of 8 or 9 inches and coat the bottom and sides with foil. Mix the rice, coconut, and butter together in a medium dish. Push the crust towards the bottom and the sides of the prepared pan somewhat upwards. When you prepare the filling, put the pan in the fridge.
2. Prepare the filling: mix together the cream cheese and sour cream in a large bowl, then whisk in the stevia and vanilla. One at a time, add the eggs, combining after each addition. Layer the filling over the crust uniformly.
3. Put the cheesecake in a deep roasting pan and set it on the oven's center rack. Pour sufficient boiling water carefully into the roasting pan to come halfway up the

spring type pan's sides. Bake for 1 hour to 1 hour 20 minutes, until the middle jiggles just slightly. Switch off the oven, but allow the cake to cool steadily for an hour in the oven with the door partially closed.

4. Remove the pan from the boiling water, remove the foil, and then let it cool for at least five hours or overnight in the refrigerator. Slice with the strawberries and garnish.

Keto Chocolate Chip Cookies

TOTAL TIME: 0 HOURS 30 MINS

YIELDS: 18

INGREDIENTS:

- 2 large size eggs
- 1/2 c (1 stick) of butter that has melted
- 2 Tbsp. of heavy milk to heavy cream
- 2 Tsp .pure extract of vanilla
- 2 3/4 c. of almond flour
- 1/4 Tsp. salt, kosher
- 1/4 c. Sugar granulated keto-friendly (such as swerve)
- 3/4 c. Chips of dark chocolate (such as lily's)
- cooking mist

DIRECTIONS

1. Preheat 350° in the oven. Mix the egg with the sugar, vanilla and heavy cream in a big dish. Add the almond flour, salt and swerve to the mixture.
2. Fold in the cookie batter with the chocolate chips. Shape the mixture into 1" balls and arrange 3" apart on baking sheets lined with parchment. Flatten the balls with cooking spray on the bottom of a glass that has been oiled.
3. Bake for around 17 to 19 minutes until the cookies are softly golden.

Keto Chocolate Mug Cake

TOTAL TIME: 0 HOURS 5 MINS

YIELDS: 1

INGREDIENTS:

- 2 Tbsp. of Butter
- 1/4 c. of almond flour
- 2 Tbsp. of powdered cocoa
- 1 large size egg, beaten
- 2 Tbsp. of chocolate chips that are keto-friendly, (such as Lily's)
- 2 Tbsp. of Swerve, Granulated
- 1/2 Tsp. of baking powder
- A pinch of Kosher salt
- For serving, whipped cream (1/4 c.)

DIRECTIONS

1. Put the butter in a microwave-safe mug and heat for 30 seconds before it is melted. Except for whipped cream, add the remaining ingredients and stir until thoroughly mixed. Cook until the cake is set, but always fudgy, for 45 seconds to 1 minute.
2. Serve with whipped cream.

Keto Ice Cream

TOTAL TIME: 8 HOURS 15 MINS

YIELDS: 8

INGREDIENT:

- 2 cans of coconut milk (15-oz.)
- 2 c. of heavy cream
- 1/4 c. Swerve the Sweetener of the Confectioner
- 1 Tsp. of pure vanilla
- A pinch of Kosher salt

DIRECTIONS

1. In the refrigerator, chill the coconut milk for at least 3 hours, preferably overnight.
2. To make whipped coconut: pour coconut cream into a big bowl, keep liquid in the bowl and beat the coconut cream until very smooth using a hand mixer. Only put back.
3. Make the whipped cream: Using a hand mixer in a separate big bowl (or a stand mixer in a bowl), beat heavy cream until soft peaks shape. Beat in the vanilla and sweetener.
4. Fold the whipped (coconut) into the whipped cream, and then add the mixture to the loaf plate.
5. Freeze for about 5 hours until it is firm.

Keto Hot Chocolate

TOTAL TIME: 0 HOURS 10 MINS

YIELDS: 1 CUP

INGREDIENTS:

- 2 Tbsp. Powder of unsweetened chocolate, and more for garnishing
- 2 1/2 Tsp. of sugar that is keto-friendly, such as Swerve
- 1 1/4 c. Aquatic Water
- 1/4 c. Heavy milk to heavy cream
- 1/4 Tsp. of pure vanilla

- Whipped(milk),for serving

DIRECTIONS:

1. Whisk together the swerve, chocolate, and about 2 teaspoons of water in a shallow pan over medium heat until smoother and dissolve. Increases heat to low, add the remaining cream and water and whisk until heated regularly.
2. Attach the vanilla, and spill it into a cup. Represent with (whipped) cream and chocolate powder dusting.

Keto Peanut Butter Cookies

TOTAL TIME: 1 HOUR 30 MINS

YIELDS: 22

INGREDIENTS

- 1 1/2c. of smooth peanut butter, unsweetened, melted (plus more for drizzling)
- 1 c. Flour of coconut
- 1/4 c. Keto-friendly brown sugar packets, such as Swerve
- 1 Tsp. of pure vanilla
- Pinch of Kosher salt
- 2 c. of melted keto-friendly dark chocolate chips, including Lily's,
- 1 Tbsp. of Cream (Coconut)
-

DIRECTIONS

1. Combine the sugar, coconut flour, peanut butter, salt, and vanilla in a medium dish. Until smooth, stir.
2. Line the parchment paper with a baking sheet. Shape the mixture into circles using a small cookie scoop, then push down gently to flatten slightly and position it on the baking sheet. Freeze until strong, roughly 1 hour.
3. Whisk the melting chocolate and coconut oil together in a medium dish.

4. Dip peanut butter rounds in chocolate using a fork until fully covered and then return to the baking sheet. Drizzle with much more peanut butter, and freeze for around 10 minutes before the chocolate is set.

5. Only serve it cold. In the fridge, put some leftovers.

Chocolate Keto Cookies

TOTAL TIME: 0 HOURS 25 MINS

YIELDS: 11

INGREDIENTS

- 2 1/2 Tbsp. of butter
- 3 Tbsp. of chocolate chips with keto, split
- 1large size egg
- 1 Tsp. of pure vanilla
- 2/3 of c. Almond Flour Blanched
- 1/3 c. of swerve Confectioners
- 3 1/2 Tbsp. Unsweetened dark chocolate powder
- 1/2 Tsp. Powder used for baking
- Pinch of Kosher salt

DIRECTIONS

1. Preheat the oven to 325 degrees. Add butter and half of the (chocolate chips) into a medium-sized dish. Microwave for 15 to 30 seconds, only enough time to melt the chocolate and butter mildly. Until a chocolate sauce emerges, mix the two together.

2. Attach and whisk the egg in a tiny dish before the yolk mixes with the whites. When it's finished, add the chocolate syrup to the bowl with the egg and vanilla extract. Again, blend.

3. To finish the cookies, add the majority of the dry ingredients, save some of the chocolate chips. Mix until it shapes a mass of chocolate cookie dough.

4. To make 11 equal-sized cookies, use a cookie spoon (or a tablespoon). Attach the cookie to a baking parchment paper and top the remainder of the chocolate chips with each cookie. In either a spoon or a spatula, flatten each cookie.
5. For 8 to 10 minutes, roast. When they come out of the oven, they should be very soft, but don't worry, this is natural!
6. Let the cookies on the baking sheet cool off. They can set up and firm up while they cool up.
7. When the leftovers are cooled, enjoy them and store them in an airtight jar in the refrigerator.

Walnut Snowball Cookies:

TOTAL TIME: 1 HOUR 5 MINS

YIELDS: 15

INGREDIENTS

- 1/2 c. (1 stick) of butter that has melted
- 1 large size egg
- 50 drops of stevia liquid (about 1/4 tsp.)
- 1/2 tsp. of pure vanilla
- 1 c. With walnuts
- 1/2 c. Flour of coconut, plus 1 or 2 tbsp. For rolling, more
- 1/2 c. of swerve Confectioners

DIRECTIONS

1. Preheat the oven to 300 ° and use parchment paper to cover a baking sheet. In a large bowl, mix the melted butter, egg, vanilla extract, stevia and set aside.
2. In a food processor, add the walnuts and pulse until ground. In a medium bowl, pour the walnut flour and add the coconut flour and 1/4 cup Swerve and press until mixed.
3. Add the dry mixture to the wet in two sections and whisk to blend. The dough should be soft but strong enough at this stage to shape hand-made balls without

sticking to your hands. If the quality is not right, add 1 to 2 tablespoons of extra (coconut) flour and mix.

4. Create 15 balls of the same size and place them on a lined baking sheet. In the microwave, they would not disperse.
5. For 30 minutes, roast.
6. Enable 5 minutes to settle, and then in the remaining 1/4 cup Swerve, roll the (still warm) spheres.
7. Put them back on the parchment paper and give another 20 to 30 minutes to cool fully before feeding.

Keto Tortilla Chips

TOTAL TIME: 0 HOURS 35 MINS

YIELDS: 4 - 6

INGREDIENTS

- 2 c. of Mozzarella cheese, Sliced
- 1 c. of almond flour
- 1 Tsp. salt, Kosher
- 1 Tsp. of garlic powder
- 1/2 Tsp. Powdered chili
- Black pepper freshly ground

DIRECTIONS

1. Preheat the oven to 350 degrees. Top the parchment paper with two wide baking sheets.
2. Melt the mozzarella in a secure microwave bowl for around 1 minute and 30 seconds. Add the almond flour, cinnamon, chili powder, garlic powder, black pepper and a few pieces. Use both hands to moisten the dough a couple of times before it forms a smooth shape.
3. Place the dough between two parchment paper sheets and stretch it out into a 1/8' wide rectangle. Break the dough into triangles using a knife or a pizza cutter.

4. Spread the chips on lined baking sheets and bake for 12 to 14 minutes until the sides are golden and begin to crisp.

Keto Burger Fat Bombs

TOTAL TIME: 0 HOURS 30 MINS

YIELDS: 20

INGREDIENTS:

- Cooking mist
- 1 lb. of meat, ground
- 1/2 tsp. powder in garlic form
- salt (kosher)
- Black pepper freshly ground
- 2 tbsp. Cold butter, 20 bits of sliced butter
- 2 oz. Split into 20 bits of cheddar,
- Lettuce berries meant for serving
- For serving, finely sliced tomatoes
- Mustard, to serve

DIRECTIONS

1. Preheat the oven to 375 °C and oil the cooking spray with a mini muffin tin. Season the beef with salt, garlic powder and pepper in a medium dish.
2. Place 1 teaspoon of beef equally, covering the bottom entirely, into the bottom of each muffin tin cup. Place a slice of butter on top and press 1 teaspoon of beef over the butter to cover full.
3. In each cup, place a slice of cheddar on top of the meat and force the remaining beef over the cheese to cover it fully.
4. Bake for about 15 minutes before the meat is ready. Let yourself cool somewhat.
5. Using a metal offset spatula carefully to release each burger out of the tin. Serve with onions, salad leaves, and mustard.

Jalapeño Popper Egg Cups

TOTAL TIME: 0 HOURS 45 MINS

YIELDS: 12

INGREDIENTS:

- 12 strips of bacon
- 10 eggs (large)
- 1/4 c. of sour milk,
- 1/2 c. Cheddar Shredded
- 1/2 c. Mozzarella Sliced
- 2(jalapeños), 1 sliced thinly and 1 finely chopped
- 1 Tsp. Powdered of garlic
- salt(kosher)
- Black pepper freshly ground
- Cooking spray, nonstick

DIRECTIONS

1. Preheat the oven to 375 degrees. Over medium heat, (cook bacon) in a broad skillet until well browned but always pliable. Put aside to drain on a paper towel-lined pan.
2. Whisk the eggs, sour cream, cheese, minced jalapeño and garlic in powder form together in a big bowl. With salt and pepper, season.
3. Oil a muffin tin with the aid of nonstick cooking oil. Line each well with one bacon strip, then pour each muffin cup with egg mixture until around two-thirds of the way through to the end. Cover each muffin with a slice of jalapeño.
4. Bake for 20 minutes until the eggs do not look moist anymore. Before withdrawing them from the muffin pan, cool slightly.

Keto Frosty

TOTAL TIME: 0 HOURS 45 MINS

YIELDS: 4

INGREDIENTS

- 1 1/2 c. Heavy cream whipping
- 2 Tbsp. Unsweetened powder of cocoa
- 3 Tbsp. Sweetener for (keto-friendly) powdered sugar, such as a Swerve
- 1 Tsp. of pure vanilla
- Pinch of Kosher salt

DIRECTIONS

1. Combine the milk, sugar, sweetener, vanilla, and salt in a wide pot. Beat the mixture until rigid peaks shape, and use a hand blender or (the whisk attachment of a stand mixer). Mix the scoops into a Ziploc container and ice for 30 to 35 minutes before they're frozen.
2. Break the tip off an edge of the Ziploc container and pour it into dishes to eat.

Bacon Guac Bombs

TOTAL TIME: 0 HOURS 45 MINS
YIELDS: 15
INGREDIENTS:

2 bacon strips, fried and crumbled

For guacamole

- 2 pitted, sliced, and mashed avocados
- 6 oz. of Cream cheese, cooked, softened
- 1 lime juice
- 1 clove of garlic, minced
- 1/4 of red onion, minced
- 1 small jalapeno (seeded if less fire is preferred), chopped
- 2 Tbsp. Cilantro, freshly sliced
- 1/2 Tsp. of cumin seeds
- 1/2 Tsp. Powdered of chili
- salt(kosher)
- Black pepper freshly ground

DIRECTIONS

1. Combine all the guacamole products in a big bowl. Stir unless mostly smooth, and add salt and pepper (some pieces are OK). Put in the freezer for 30 minutes to firm up rapidly.

2. On a wide tray, put crumbled bacon. Scoop the guacamole mix and put in the bacon, utilizing a little cookie scoop. Roll in the bacon to coat. Repeat before you've used both the bacon and guacamole. Store in refrigerator.

Avocado Chips

TOTAL TIME: 0 HOURS 40 MINS
YIELDS: 15
INGREDIENTS

- 1 large ripe avocado
- 3/4 c. Freshly grated parmesan
- 1 tsp. Lemon juice
- 1/2 tsp. Garlic powder
- 1/2 tsp. Italian seasoning
- Kosher salt

- Freshly ground black pepper

DIRECTIONS

1. Preheat oven to 325° and line two baking sheets with parchment paper. In a medium bowl, mash avocado with a fork until smooth. Stir in parmesan, lemon juice, garlic powder, and Italian seasoning. Season with salt and pepper.
2. Place heaping teaspoon-size scoops of mixture on baking sheet, leaving about 3″ apart between each scoop. Flatten each scoop to 3″ wide across with the back of a spoon or measuring cup. Bake until crisp and golden, about 30 minutes, then let cool completely. Serve at room temperature.

Rosemary Keto Crackers

TOTAL TIME: 1 HOUR 0 MINS
YIELDS: 140
INGREDIENTS

- 2 1/2 c. almond flour
- 1/2 c. coconut flour
- 1 tsp. ground flaxseed meal
- 1/2 tsp. dried rosemary, chopped
- 1/2 tsp. onion powder
- 1/4 tsp. kosher salt
- 3 large eggs
- 1 tbsp. extra-virgin olive oil

DIRECTIONS

1. Preheat oven to 325° and line a baking sheet with parchment paper. In a large bowl, whisk together flours, flaxmeal, rosemary, onion powder, and salt. Add eggs and oil and mix to combine. Continue mixing until dough forms a large ball, about 1 minute.
2. Sandwich dough between 2 pieces of parchment and roll to ¼″ thick. Cut into squares and transfer to prepared baking sheet.
3. Bake until golden, 12 to 15 minutes. Let cool before storing in a resalable container.

Conclusion

A ketogenic diet could be an alternative for certain people who have experienced trouble losing weight with other approaches. The exact ratio of fat, carbohydrate, and protein that is required to attain health benefits can differ among individuals due to their genetic makeup and body structure. Therefore, if one decides to start a ketogenic diet, it is advised to meet with one's physician and a dietitian to closely track any metabolic adjustments since beginning the treatment and to develop a meal schedule that is specific to one's current health problems and to avoid food shortages or other health risks. A dietitian can also have advice on reintroducing carbs after weight reduction is accomplished.

CPSIA information can be obtained
at www.ICGtesting.com
Printed in the USA
BVHW011737090321
602113BV00016B/1833